The Proverbial Marquee

Words To Drive By

Tina Rabb

and

Deborah Davies

CSS Publishing Company, Inc., Lima, Ohio

THE PROVERBIAL MARQUEE

Copyright © 2001 by
CSS Publishing Company, Inc.
Lima, Ohio

Some scripture references are from the *Holy Bible, New International Version*. Copyright © 1973, 1978, 1984 International Bible Society. Used by permission of Zondervan Bible Publishers. All rights reserved.

Some scripture quotations are from the *King James Version of the Bible*, in the public domain.

Library of Congress Cataloging-in-Publication Data

Rabb, Tina, 1955-
    The proverbial marquee : words to drive by / Tina Rabb and Deborah Davies.
      p.   cm.
    ISBN 0-7880-1801-9 (alk. paper)
    1. Church signs. 2. Proverbs, English. I. Davies, Deborah, 1958- II. Title.
BV653.7 .R33 2001
254'.4—dc21   00-065119
                                                     CIP

For more information about CSS Publishing Company resources, visit our website at www.csspub.com.

ISBN 0-7880-1801-9   PRINTED IN U.S.A.

To Rob and Joe,
who always said we could do
whatever we wanted to

Introduction

There are probably more than a million church marquees in the United States, each offering an unparalleled chance to promote the kingdom of Christ. How sad when, instead, passersby are greeted with muddled and downright offensive messages, some made even worse with spelling and punctuation errors. *The Proverbial Marquee: Words To Drive By* is a cure for what's ailing so many church marquees today. It's a complete collection of both proven proverbs (including scripture) and original wisdoms, all especially suited to signage. While there are several good Christian quote collections available, *The Proverbial Marquee* is a unique church resource in several ways:

- Sayings are categorized for quick reference.
- Each message is formatted line by line for easy drive-by reading.
- Line lengths are calculated to fall well within the average church sign's width.
- Best of all, a convenient letter count is provided.

With more than 700 messages divided among thirty categories, *The Proverbial Marquee* provides enough material to make and keep your church marquee a city-wide focal point for years to come. It's our hope that this little book blesses, exhorts, and inspires both your congregation and your entire community.

Your marquee can be a bright light in a dark world. Let it shine!

Tina Rabb and Deborah Davies

Sample

THE SOUL IS HEALED
BY BEING WITH
CHILDREN.
— DOSTOYEVSKY
    [.]1 [A]1 [B]2 [C]1 [D]2 [E]5 [G]1 [H]4 [I]4
    [L]3 [N]2 [O]1 [R]1 [S]2 [T]2 [U]1 [W]1 [Y]1
    [D]1 [E]1 [K]1 [O]2 [S]2 [T]1 [V]1 [Y]2 [—]1

Note: For easiest drive-by readability, follow the suggested line breaks. The letters needed for the message are listed in brackets with the number of each letter listed after the bracket. Two alphabetical lines of letter count appear after each message. Where an author is identified with the message, a third line of letter count is included. (Letter counts for *Wings Of Silver* and *God's Little Instruction Book* are not included.)

Table Of Contents

Marquee Suggestions

How to use marquee messages

• No matter how much you like a particular marquee message, try not to reuse it for at least two years. (To save yourself some bother down the road, note the day you use each marquee message.)

• Change your marquee *at least* once a week. Your drive-by congregation is probably more aware of your marquee than you realize, and you don't want your message to get old.

• Consider changing your marquee twice a week. You might make one of the semi-weekly messages a proverb and the other an announcement of an upcoming church activity. Yes, changing the sign is time-consuming, but well worth your effort. Just think how many hours a minister invests in preparing a sermon that will reach a few hundred people. Marquees, even those with limited exposure, can easily reach thousands.

• Include in your marquee announcements of any and every church function. Your community finds an active church more vital and, ultimately, more attractive.

• Hosting a mother-daughter tea? Marquee it!

• Having a father-son function? Marquee it!

• Special speaker coming? Marquee it! (And include his or her topic or specialty.)

• Cooking up a covered-dish dinner? The way to a community could be through its stomach, so marquee the time and place!

• Has your children's program added a new puppet? Tell the kids to come meet her this Sunday.

• Don't be afraid to come up with your own marquee messages. But beware. Just because you have a line you love — and could even use effectively with the home congregation — doesn't mean it's appropriate for public consumption. Test: Does it speak the truth in love?

• The dictionary is our friend! Consider keeping a pocket-sized version with your marquee letters. Believe it or not, passersby *will* judge you by the spelling on your marquee.

• Whatever you do, don't leave your board blank. A marquee without a message tells the community your church is at a loss.

• Be sensitive about not only the content but also the timing of your messages. One church put up the message "Be sure you don't expire before your driver's license does," the day before the church next door held a funeral for a seventeen-year-old killed in an auto accident. Fortunately, the message was removed just before the funeral started.

• When it comes to the effort your church marquee requires, remember Galatians 6:9 — "... [D]o not be weary in well-doing." Some who wouldn't dream of attending a church will religiously read your marquee.

• Invest in your marquee alphabet. Jesus multiplied the loaves and fish in order for all to be fed, so have plenty of letters on hand to feed your drive-by multitudes.

• Sermon titles oftentimes make good marquee messages.

• Remember, it's:
Their church is over *there*.
You're doing a good job with *your* marquee.
It's great when a church uses *its* marquee.

• Your marquee tells your community who you are. Don't use a message from this or any other book that isn't an accurate reflection of your church's theology.

• One more reason to change your marquee often: The longer your audience has to look at a maxim, the more callused they may become to it. Skeptics in particular will use every passing to raise up another barrier to your message.

• If you've got a great marquee message to share, email it (along with its source) to momsters@argontech.net.

• Faith comes by the word, so be sure your marquee uses scripture plentifully.

• Use marquee messages on classroom bulletin boards and as fillers in church bulletins.

The Proverbial Marquee

Words To Drive By

A Joy Ride

Happy hints for staying on the sunny side

**SHARED JOY
IS A
DOUBLE JOY.**
[.]1 [A]2 [B]1 [D]2 [E]2 [H]1 [I]1
[J]2 [L]1 [O]3 [R]1 [S]2 [U]1 [Y]2

**AMAZING GRACE.
ABOUNDING JOY.
ABUNDANT LOVE.**
[.]3 [A]6 [B]2 [C]1 [D]2 [E]2 [G]3 [I]2 [J]1
[L]1 [M]1 [N]5 [O]3 [R]1 [T]1 [U]2 [V]1 [Y]1 [Z]1

**HE LAUGHS BEST
WHO LAUGHS OFTEN.**
[.]1 [A]2 [B]1 [E]3 [F]1 [G]2 [H]4
[L]2 [N]1 [O]2 [S]3 [T]2 [U]2 [W]1

**A SMILE
CONFUSES AN
APPROACHING FROWN.
— ANONYMOUS**
[.]1 [A]4 [C]2 [E]2 [F]2 [G]1 [H]1 [I]2
[L]1 [M]1 [N]4 [O]3 [P]2 [R]2 [S]3 [U]1 [W]1
[A]1 [M]1 [N]2 [O]2 [S]1 [U]1 [Y]1 [—]1

**THE KINGDOM
OF GOD IS
RIGHTEOUSNESS,
PEACE, AND JOY.**

[,]2 [.]1 [A]2 [C]1 [D]3 [E]5 [F]1 [G]3 [H]2 [I]3
[J]1 [K]1 [M]1 [N]3 [O]5 [P]1 [R]1 [S]4 [T]2 [U]1 [Y]1

**LIVE WELL,
LAUGH OFTEN,
LOVE MUCH. — ANONYMOUS**

[,]2 [.]1 [A]1 [C]1 [E]4 [F]1 [G]1 [H]2
[I]1 [L]5 [M]1 [N]1 [O]2 [T]1 [U]2 [V]2 [W]1
[A]1 [M]1 [N]2 [O]2 [S]1 [U]1 [Y]1 [—]1

GOT MILK 'N' HONEY?

[']1 [']1 [?]1 [E]1 [G]1 [H]1 [I]1
[K]1 [L]1 [M]1 [N]2 [O]2 [T]1 [Y]1

**HAPPINESS IS
A WAY OF TRAVEL,
NOT A DESTINATION.
— ROY GOODMAN**

[,]1 [.]1 [A]6 [D]1 [E]3 [F]1 [H]1 [I]4 [L]1
[N]4 [O]3 [P]2 [R]1 [S]4 [T]4 [V]1 [W]1 [Y]1
[A]1 [D]1 [G]1 [M]1 [N]1 [O]3 [R]1 [Y]1 [—]1

**NO MAN IS MORE
UNHAPPY THAN HE
WHO IS NEVER IN
ADVERSITY. — ANONYMOUS**

[.]1 [A]4 [D]1 [E]5 [H]4 [I]4 [M]2 [N]6
[O]3 [P]2 [R]3 [S]3 [T]2 [U]1 [V]2 [W]1 [Y]2
[A]1 [M]1 [N]2 [O]2 [S]1 [U]1 [Y]1 [—]1

**TURN YOUR FACE TO
THE SUN AND THE
SHADOWS FALL BEHIND
YOU. — MAORI PROVERB**

[.]1 [A]4 [B]1 [C]1 [D]3 [E]4 [F]2 [H]4 [I]1
[L]2 [N]4 [O]4 [R]2 [S]3 [T]4 [U]4 [W]1 [Y]2
[A]1 [B]1 [E]1 [I]1 [M]1 [O]2 [P]1 [R]3 [V]1 [—]1

**WANNA FEEL RICH?
COUNT EVERYTHING YOU
HAVE THAT MONEY
CAN'T BUY. — ANONYMOUS**

[']1 [.]1 [?]1 [A]5 [B]1 [C]3 [E]6 [F]1 [G]1 [H]4
[I]2 [L]1 [M]1 [N]6 [O]3 [R]2 [T]5 [U]3 [V]2 [W]1 [Y]4
[A]1 [M]1 [N]2 [O]2 [S]1 [U]1 [Y]1 [—]1

**THE TRUTH WILL
SET YOU FREE.
IT JUST WON'T ALWAYS
MAKE YOU HAPPY.**

[']1 [.]2 [A]4 [E]5 [F]1 [H]3 [I]2 [J]1 [K]1 [L]3
[M]1 [N]1 [O]3 [P]2 [R]2 [S]3 [T]7 [U]4 [W]3 [Y]4

**PRACTICE AN ATTITUDE
OF GRATITUDE.**
(*Wings of Silver*)

[.]1 [A]4 [C]2 [D]2 [E]3 [F]1 [G]1
[I]3 [N]1 [O]1 [P]1 [R]2 [T]6 [U]2

19

HAPPINESS IS A
BY-PRODUCT OF TRYING
TO MAKE SOMEONE ELSE
HAPPY. — GRETTA PALMER

[-]1 [.]1 [A]4 [B]1 [C]1 [D]1 [E]6 [F]1 [G]1 [H]2 [I]3
[K]1 [L]1 [M]2 [N]3 [O]5 [P]5 [R]2 [S]5 [T]3 [U]1 [Y]3
[A]2 [E]2 [G]1 [L]1 [M]1 [P]1 [R]2 [T]2 [—]1

SMILES:
STILL WORKING ON
YOUR FIRST MILLION?

[:]1 [?]1 [E]1 [F]1 [G]1 [I]6 [K]1 [L]5
[M]2 [N]3 [O]4 [R]3 [S]4 [T]2 [U]1 [W]1 [Y]1

THE SOUL IS HEALED
BY BEING WITH
CHILDREN.
— DOSTOYEVSKY

[.]1 [A]1 [B]2 [C]1 [D]2 [E]5 [G]1 [H]4 [I]4
[L]3 [N]2 [O]1 [R]1 [S]2 [T]2 [U]1 [W]1 [Y]1
[D]1 [E]1 [K]1 [O]2 [S]2 [T]1 [V]1 [Y]2 [—]1

CAN'T SLEEP?
COUNT BLESSINGS.

[']1 [.]1 [?]1 [A]1 [B]1 [C]2 [E]3 [G]1
[I]1 [L]2 [N]3 [O]1 [P]1 [S]4 [T]2 [U]1

UNHAPPINESS STARTS
WITH WANTING
TO BE HAPPIER.
— SAM LEVENSON

[.]1 [A]4 [B]1 [E]3 [G]1 [H]3 [I]4
[N]4 [O]1 [P]4 [R]2 [S]4 [T]5 [U]1 [W]2
[A]1 [E]2 [L]1 [M]1 [N]2 [O]1 [S]2 [V]1 [—]1

IF YOU'RE HAPPY
AND YOU KNOW IT,
HONK YOUR HORN.

[']1 [,]1 [.]1 [A]2 [D]1 [E]1 [F]1 [H]3 [I]2
[K]2 [N]4 [O]6 [P]2 [R]3 [T]1 [U]3 [W]1 [Y]4

SPECIAL TODAY:
3 FOR 1 —
PEACE, JOY, LOVE

[,]2 [—]1 [1]1 [3]1 [:]1 [A]3 [C]2 [D]1 [E]4 [F]1
[I]1 [J]1 [L]2 [O]4 [P]2 [R]1 [S]1 [T]1 [V]1 [Y]2

JOY IS THE
SERIOUS BUSINESS
OF HEAVEN.
— C. S. LEWIS

[.]1 [A]1 [B]1 [E]5 [F]1 [H]2 [I]3 [J]1
[N]2 [O]3 [R]1 [S]6 [T]1 [U]2 [V]1 [Y]1
[.]2 [C]1 [E]1 [I]1 [L]1 [S]2 [W]1 [—]1

JESUS' SUFFERING
HAS FREED US FOR
JOYFUL OBEDIENCE.

[']1 [.]1 [A]1 [B]1 [C]1 [D]2 [E]7 [F]5 [G]1
[H]1 [I]2 [J]2 [L]1 [N]2 [O]3 [R]3 [S]5 [U]4 [Y]1

21

A Ration Of Compassion

Maxims of mercy

**SYMPATHY: TWO HEARTS
TUGGING AT ONE LOAD.
— CHARLES H. PACKHURST**

[.]1 [:]1 [A]4 [D]1 [E]2 [G]3 [H]2 [I]1 [L]1
[M]1 [N]2 [O]3 [P]1 [R]1 [S]2 [T]5 [U]1 [W]1 [Y]2
[.]1 [A]2 [C]2 [E]1 [H]3 [K]1 [L]1 [P]1 [R]2 [S]2 [T]1 [U]1 [—]1

**CARE AND
CARE ALIKE.**

[.]1 [A]4 [C]2 [D]1 [E]3 [I]1 [K]1 [L]1 [N]1 [R]2

**REMEMBER THOSE WHO ARE
SUFFERING AS IF YOU
WERE SUFFERING WITH
THEM. — HEBREWS 13:3**

[—]1 [.]1 [1]1 [3]2 [:]1 [A]2 [B]2 [E]12 [F]5 [G]2
[H]5 [I]4 [M]3 [N]2 [O]3 [R]7 [S]5 [T]3 [U]3 [W]4 [Y]1

**CARRY EACH OTHER'S
BURDENS, AND YOU WILL
FULFILL THE LAW
OF CHRIST. — GALATIANS 6:2**

[']1 [,]1 [—]1 [.]1 [2]1 [6]1 [:]1 [A]7 [B]1 [C]3 [D]2 [E]4
[F]3 [G]1 [H]4 [I]4 [L]7 [N]3 [O]3 [R]5 [S]4 [T]4 [U]3 [W]2 [Y]2

**SORROW SHARED
IS SORROW HALVED.**
[.]1 [A]2 [D]2 [E]2 [H]2 [I]1
[L]1 [O]4 [R]5 [S]4 [V]1 [W]2

**WHATEVER MEASURE YOU
DEAL OUT TO OTHERS
WILL BE DEALT TO YOU
IN RETURN. — LUKE 6:38**
[—]1 [.]1 [3]1 [6]1 [8]1 [:]1 [A]4 [B]1 [D]2 [E]10 [H]2 [I]2
[K]1 [L]5 [M]1 [N]2 [O]6 [R]5 [S]2 [T]7 [U]6 [V]1 [W]2 [Y]2

**YOU CANNOT
SHAKE HANDS
WITH A CLENCHED FIST.
— GOLDA MEIR**
[.]1 [A]4 [C]3 [D]2 [E]3 [F]1 [H]4 [I]2
[K]1 [L]1 [N]4 [O]2 [S]3 [T]3 [U]1 [W]1 [Y]1
[A]1 [D]1 [E]1 [G]1 [I]1 [L]1 [M]1 [O]1 [R]1 [—]1

**MERCY HAS NO
EXPIRATION DATE.**
[.]1 [A]3 [C]1 [D]1 [E]3 [H]1 [I]2 [M]1
[N]2 [O]2 [P]1 [R]2 [S]1 [T]2 [X]1 [Y]1

**YOU MAY GIVE WITHOUT
LOVING, BUT YOU CANNOT
LOVE WITHOUT GIVING.**
(*Wings of Silver*)
[,]1 [.]1 [A]2 [B]1 [C]1 [E]2 [G]4 [H]2 [I]6
[L]2 [M]1 [N]4 [O]7 [T]6 [U]5 [V]4 [W]2 [Y]3

**IT DOESN'T MATTER
WHERE YOU ARE AS
LONG AS YOUR HEART'S
IN THE RIGHT PLACE.**
[']2 [.]1 [A]6 [C]1 [D]1 [E]8 [G]2 [H]4 [I]3 [L]2
[M]1 [N]3 [O]4 [P]1 [R]6 [S]4 [T]7 [U]2 [W]1 [Y]2

**FREELY YE
HAVE RECEIVED,
FREELY GIVE.
— MATTHEW 10:8**
[,]1 [—]1 [.]1 [0]1 [1]1 [8]1 [:]1 [A]2 [C]1 [D]1 [E]11
[F]2 [G]1 [H]2 [I]2 [L]2 [M]1 [R]3 [T]2 [V]3 [W]1 [Y]3

**A LABOR OF LOVE
WILL EVENTUALLY
PAY FOR ITSELF.**
[.]1 [A]4 [B]1 [E]4 [F]3 [I]2 [L]7 [N]1
[O]4 [P]1 [R]2 [S]1 [T]2 [U]1 [V]2 [W]1 [Y]2

**WE THEN THAT ARE STRONG
OUGHT TO BEAR THE
INFIRMITIES OF THE
WEAK. — ROMANS 15:1**
[—]1 [.]1 [1]2 [5]1 [:]1 [A]5 [B]1 [E]8 [F]2 [G]2
[H]5 [I]4 [K]1 [M]2 [N]4 [O]5 [R]5 [S]3 [T]9 [U]1 [W]2

At The Heart Of The Matter

Because what the world needs now is love, his love

IF YOU JUDGE PEOPLE,
YOU HAVE NO TIME
TO LOVE THEM.
— MOTHER TERESA
[,]1 [.]1 [A]1 [D]1 [E]7 [F]1 [G]1 [H]2 [I]2
[J]1 [L]2 [M]2 [N]1 [O]6 [P]2 [T]3 [U]3 [V]2 [Y]2
[A]1 [E]3 [H]1 [M]1 [O]1 [R]2 [S]1 [T]2 [—]1

LOVE IS A FLAME.
COME ADD FUEL
TO THE FIRE.
[.]2 [A]3 [C]1 [D]2 [E]6 [F]3 [H]1 [I]2
[L]3 [M]2 [O]3 [R]1 [S]1 [T]2 [U]1 [V]1

HE DOES MUCH
WHO LOVES MUCH.
— THOMAS À KEMPIS
[.]1 [C]2 [D]1 [E]3 [H]4 [L]1 [M]2 [O]3 [S]2 [U]2 [V]1 [W]1
[A]2 [E]1 [H]1 [I]1 [K]1 [M]2 [O]1 [P]1 [S]2 [T]1 [—]1

LOVE WILL COVER
A MULTITUDE
OF SINS.
— 1 PETER 4:8
[—]1 [.]1 [1]1 [4]1 [8]1 [:]1 [A]1 [C]1 [D]1 [E]5 [F]1
[I]3 [L]4 [M]1 [N]1 [O]3 [P]1 [R]2 [S]2 [T]3 [U]2 [V]2 [W]1

NOTHING BEATS LOVE AT
FIRST SIGHT EXCEPT
LOVE WITH INSIGHT.
(*Wings of Silver*)
    [.]1 [A]2 [B]1 [C]1 [E]5 [F]1 [G]3 [H]4 [I]6
    [L]2 [N]3 [O]3 [P]1 [R]1 [S]4 [T]8 [V]2 [W]1 [X]1

LOVE IS
A MATTER OF TIMING.
WE NEED IT
ALL THE TIME.
    [.]2 [A]3 [D]1 [E]7 [F]1 [G]1 [H]1 [I]5
    [L]3 [M]3 [N]2 [O]2 [R]1 [S]1 [T]6 [V]1 [W]1

WHERE THERE IS
GREAT LOVE, THERE ARE
ALWAYS MIRACLES.
— WILLA CATHER
    [,]1 [.]1 [A]5 [C]1 [E]10 [G]1 [H]3 [I]2
    [L]3 [M]1 [O]1 [R]6 [S]3 [T]3 [V]1 [W]2 [Y]1
    [A]2 [C]1 [E]1 [H]1 [I]1 [L]2 [R]1 [T]1 [W]1 [—]1

HE LOVES YOU,
HE LOVES YOU A LOT.
HE LOVES YOU,
HE LOVES YOU A LOT.
    [,]2 [.]2 [A]2 [E]8 [H]4 [L]6 [O]10 [S]4 [T]2 [U]4 [V]4 [Y]4

HEY, YOU!
ARE!
LOVED!
    [!]3 [,]1 [A]1 [D]1 [E]3 [H]1
    [L]1 [O]2 [R]1 [U]1 [V]1 [Y]2

HE LOVES BEST
WHO FIRST LOVED US.
[.]1 [B]1 [D]1 [E]4 [F]1 [H]2 [I]1
[L]2 [O]3 [R]1 [S]4 [T]2 [U]1 [V]2 [W]1

GOD IS LOVE.
— 1 JOHN 4:8
[—]1 [.]1 [1]1 [4]1 [8]1 [:]1 [D]1 [E]1
[G]1 [H]1 [I]1 [J]1 [L]1 [N]1 [O]3 [S]1 [V]1

YOU ARE LOVED.
NO QUESTIONS ASKED.
[.]2 [A]2 [D]2 [E]4 [I]1 [K]1 [L]1 [N]2
[O]4 [Q]1 [R]1 [S]3 [T]1 [U]2 [V]1 [Y]1

KNOWLEDGE PUFFS UP,
BUT LOVE BUILDS UP.
[,]1 [.]1 [B]2 [D]2 [E]3 [F]2 [G]1 [I]1 [K]1
[L]3 [N]1 [O]2 [P]3 [S]2 [T]1 [U]5 [V]1 [W]1

ABIDE IN LOVE.
AND WHILE
YOU'RE THERE,
LOOK UP JOY & PEACE.
[&]1 [']1 [,]1 [.]2 [A]3 [B]1 [C]1 [D]2 [E]8 [H]2 [I]3
[J]1 [K]1 [L]3 [N]2 [O]5 [P]2 [R]2 [T]1 [U]2 [V]1 [W]1 [Y]2

REAL LOVE DOESN'T
EXCUSE; IT EXHORTS.
[']1 [.]1 [;]1 [A]1 [C]1 [D]1 [E]6 [H]1 [I]1
[L]2 [N]1 [O]3 [R]2 [S]3 [T]3 [U]1 [V]1 [X]2

WHAT IS LOVE?
THE OPPOSITE OF
INTOLERANCE.
    [.]1 [?]1 [A]2 [C]1 [E]5 [F]1 [H]2 [I]3
    [L]2 [N]2 [O]5 [P]2 [R]1 [S]2 [T]4 [V]1 [W]1

WITH GOD,
EVEN THOSE WITH
BROKEN HEARTS CAN
LOVE WHOLEHEARTEDLY.
    [,]1 [.]1 [A]3 [B]1 [C]1 [D]2 [E]9 [G]1 [H]6 [I]2
    [K]1 [L]3 [N]3 [O]5 [R]3 [S]2 [T]5 [V]2 [W]3 [Y]1

LOVE RUNS
IN THE FAMILY.
    [.]1 [A]1 [E]2 [F]1 [H]1 [I]2 [L]2 [M]1
    [N]2 [O]1 [R]1 [S]1 [T]1 [U]1 [V]1 [Y]1

LOVE IS A FIRE.
FAN THE FLAMES.
    [.]2 [A]3 [E]4 [F]3 [H]1 [I]2 [L]2
    [M]1 [N]1 [O]1 [R]1 [S]2 [T]1 [V]1

YES,
JESUS LOVES YOU.
    [,]1 [.]1 [E]3 [J]1 [L]1 [O]2 [S]4 [U]2 [V]1 [Y]2

LOVE HEALS.
(*Wings of Silver*)
    [.]1 [A]1 [E]2 [H]1 [L]2 [O]1 [S]1 [V]1

**GOD CANNOT LODGE
IN A NARROW HEART.**
— ANONYMOUS
    [.]1 [A]4 [C]1 [D]2 [E]2 [G]2 [H]1
    [I]1 [L]1 [N]4 [O]4 [R]3 [T]2 [W]1
    [A]1 [M]1 [N]2 [O]2 [S]1 [U]1 [Y]1 [—]1

**WE LOVE
BECAUSE GOD
FIRST LOVED US.**
— 1 JOHN 4:19
    [—]1 [.]1 [1]2 [4]1 [9]1 [:]1 [A]1 [B]1 [C]1 [D]2 [E]5 [F]1 [G]1
    [H]1 [I]1 [J]1 [L]2 [N]1 [O]4 [R]1 [S]3 [T]1 [U]2 [V]2 [W]1

Blessed Are They With Many Letters

*Long-winded wisdoms for those with an ample
alphabet set and a sizable sign*

JESUS WENT UP, SO THE
SPIRIT COULD COME
DOWN, SO THE CHURCH
COULD GO OUT.
— LARRY ALLGOOD
[,]2 [.]1 [C]5 [D]3 [E]5 [G]1 [H]4 [I]2 [J]1
[L]2 [M]1 [N]2 [O]8 [P]2 [R]2 [S]5 [T]5 [U]6 [W]2
[A]2 [D]1 [G]1 [L]3 [O]2 [R]2 [Y]1 [—]1

IT'S NOT WHAT WE CHRISTIANS
TELL OTHERS ABOUT LIFE BUT
WHAT OUR LIVES TELL
OTHERS ABOUT CHRISTIANS.
[']1 [.]1 [A]6 [B]3 [C]2 [E]7 [F]1 [H]6 [I]7
[L]6 [N]3 [O]6 [R]5 [S]8 [T]13 [U]4 [V]1 [W]3

OUR SERVICES ARE
PEACEFUL ENOUGH FOR
THE PARENTS, CAPTIVATING
ENOUGH FOR THE KIDS.
[,]1 [.]1 [A]5 [C]3 [D]1 [E]10 [F]3 [G]3 [H]4 [I]4
[K]1 [L]1 [N]4 [O]5 [P]3 [R]6 [S]4 [T]5 [U]4 [V]2

**ALL MEN WHO LIVE
WITH ANY DEGREE OF
SERENITY LIVE BY SOME
ASSURANCE OF GRACE.
— REINHOLD NIEBUHR**

[.]1 [A]5 [B]1 [C]2 [D]1 [E]11 [F]2 [G]2 [H]2 [I]4
[L]4 [M]2 [N]4 [O]4 [R]4 [S]4 [T]2 [U]1 [V]2 [W]2 [Y]3
[B]1 [D]1 [E]2 [H]2 [I]2 [L]1 [N]2 [O]1 [R]2 [U]1 [—]1

**IT IS NOT FAIR TO ASK
OF OTHERS WHAT YOU ARE
NOT WILLING TO DO
YOURSELF. — ELEANOR ROOSEVELT**

[.]1 [A]4 [D]1 [E]3 [F]3 [G]1 [H]2 [I]5 [K]1
[L]3 [N]3 [O]9 [R]4 [S]4 [T]7 [U]2 [W]2 [Y]2
[A]1 [E]4 [L]2 [N]1 [O]3 [R]2 [S]1 [T]1 [V]1 [—]1

**YOU'RE ONLY YOUNG
ONCE, BUT YOU CAN
STAY IMMATURE
INDEFINITELY. — ANONYMOUS**

[']1 [,]1 [.]1 [A]3 [B]1 [C]2 [D]1 [E]5 [F]1 [G]1
[I]4 [L]2 [M]2 [N]6 [O]5 [R]2 [S]1 [T]4 [U]5 [Y]6
[A]1 [M]1 [N]2 [O]2 [S]1 [U]1 [Y]1 [—]1

**SUCCESS IN MARRIAGE
ISN'T ABOUT FINDING
THE RIGHT PERSON — IT'S
ABOUT BEING THE RIGHT
PERSON. — ANONYMOUS**

[']2 [—]1 [.]1 [A]4 [B]3 [C]2 [D]1 [E]7 [F]1 [G]5
[H]4 [I]9 [M]1 [N]7 [O]4 [P]2 [R]6 [S]7 [T]8 [U]3
[A]1 [M]1 [N]2 [O]2 [S]1 [U]1 [Y]1 [—]1

**EAT A LIVE FROG IN THE
MORNING, AND NOTHING
WORSE WILL HAPPEN TO
EITHER OF YOU THE
REST OF THE DAY. — ANONYMOUS**

[,]1 [.]1 [A]5 [D]2 [E]10 [F]3 [G]3 [H]6 [I]6 [L]3
[M]1 [N]7 [O]8 [P]2 [R]5 [S]2 [T]8 [U]1 [V]1 [W]2 [Y]2
[A]1 [M]1 [N]2 [O]2 [S]1 [U]1 [Y]1 [—]1

**THE MAIN OBJECT OF RELIGION
IS NOT TO GET A MAN INTO
HEAVEN, BUT TO GET HEAVEN
INTO HIM. — THOMAS HARDY**

[,]1 [.]1 [A]5 [B]2 [C]1 [E]9 [F]1 [G]3 [H]4 [I]7
[J]1 [L]1 [M]3 [N]8 [O]8 [R]1 [S]1 [T]10 [U]1 [V]2
[A]2 [D]1 [H]2 [M]1 [O]1 [R]1 [S]1 [T]1 [Y]1 [—]1

**BE TENDER WITH THE YOUNG,
COMPASSIONATE WITH THE AGED,
SYMPATHETIC WITH THE STRIVING.
— REVISED GEORGE W. CARVER**

[,]2 [.]1 [A]4 [B]1 [C]2 [D]2 [E]9 [G]3 [H]7 [I]7
[M]2 [N]4 [O]3 [P]2 [R]2 [S]4 [T]11 [U]1 [V]1 [W]3 [Y]2
[.]1 [A]1 [C]1 [D]1 [E]5 [G]2 [I]1 [O]1 [R]4 [S]1 [V]2 [W]1 [—]1

**THE BEST PORTION OF A GOOD
MAN'S LIFE IS HIS LITTLE,
NAMELESS, UNREMEMBERED
ACTS OF KINDNESS AND OF
LOVE. — WORDSWORTH**

[']1 [,]2 [.]1 [A]5 [B]2 [C]1 [D]4 [E]12 [F]4 [G]1 [H]2
[I]6 [K]1 [L]5 [M]4 [N]7 [O]8 [P]1 [R]3 [S]9 [T]6 [U]1 [V]1
[D]1 [H]1 [O]2 [R]2 [S]1 [T]1 [W]2 [—]1

**WE BROUGHT NOTHING
INTO THIS WORLD. AND IT
IS CERTAIN WE CARRY
NOTHING OUT OF IT.
— 1 TIMOTHY 6:7**
 [—]1 [.]2 [1]1 [6]1 [7]1 [:]1 [A]3 [B]1 [C]2 [D]2 [E]3 [F]1 [G]3
 [H]5 [I]9 [L]1 [M]1 [N]7 [O]8 [R]5 [S]2 [T]11 [U]2 [W]3 [Y]2

**ONE THING YOU WILL
PROBABLY REMEMBER WELL
IS ANY TIME YOU
FORGIVE AND FORGET.
— FRANKLIN P. JONES**
 [.]1 [A]3 [B]3 [D]1 [E]8 [F]2 [G]3 [H]1 [I]5 [L]5
 [M]3 [N]4 [O]6 [P]1 [R]5 [S]1 [T]3 [U]2 [V]1 [W]2 [Y]4
 [.]1 [A]1 [E]1 [F]1 [I]1 [J]1 [K]1 [L]1 [N]3 [O]1 [P]1 [R]1 [S]1 [—]1

**YOU CANNOT DO A KINDNESS
TOO SOON, FOR YOU NEVER
KNOW HOW SOON IT WILL
BE TOO LATE. — EMERSON**
 [,]1 [.]1 [A]3 [B]1 [C]1 [D]2 [E]5 [F]1 [H]1 [I]3
 [K]2 [L]3 [N]8 [O]15 [R]2 [S]4 [T]5 [U]2 [V]1 [W]3 [Y]2
 [E]2 [M]1 [N]1 [O]1 [R]1 [S]1 [—]1

**THERE IS SOME GOOD IN
THE WORST OF US AND
SOME EVIL IN THE BEST
OF US. — M. L. KING, JR.**
 [.]1 [A]1 [B]1 [D]2 [E]8 [F]2 [G]1 [H]3 [I]4
 [L]1 [M]2 [N]3 [O]7 [R]2 [S]7 [T]5 [U]2 [V]1 [W]1
 [,]1 [.]3 [G]1 [I]1 [J]1 [K]1 [L]1 [M]1 [N]1 [R]1 [—]1

**HAVE A HEART THAT NEVER
HARDENS, A TEMPER THAT
NEVER TRIES, A TOUCH
THAT NEVER HURTS. — DICKENS**

[,]2 [.]1 [A]9 [C]1 [D]1 [E]12 [H]8 [I]1
[M]1 [N]4 [O]1 [P]1 [R]8 [S]3 [T]11 [U]2 [V]4
[C]1 [D]1 [E]1 [I]1 [K]1 [N]1 [S]1 [—]1

**THOUGH THOU HAST EVER
SO MANY COUNSELORS,
YET DO NOT FORSAKE
THE COUNSEL OF YOUR
SOUL. — JOHN RAY**

[,]1 [.]1 [A]3 [C]2 [D]1 [E]7 [F]2 [G]1 [H]5 [K]1
[L]3 [M]1 [N]4 [O]12 [R]4 [S]7 [T]6 [U]6 [V]1 [Y]3
[A]1 [H]1 [J]1 [N]1 [O]1 [R]1 [Y]1 [—]1

**WORRY IS LIKE A
ROCKING CHAIR.
IT GIVES YOU SOMETHING
TO DO BUT DOESN'T
GET YOU ANYWHERE.**
(*Wings of Silver*)

[']1 [.]2 [A]3 [B]1 [C]2 [D]2 [E]7 [G]4 [H]3 [I]7 [K]2
[L]1 [M]1 [N]4 [O]8 [R]5 [S]4 [T]6 [U]3 [V]1 [W]2 [Y]4

**THE ONE WHO SAYS IT
CANNOT BE DONE SHOULD
NEVER INTERRUPT THE
ONE WHO IS DOING IT.
— ANONYMOUS**

[.]1 [A]2 [B]1 [C]1 [D]3 [E]9 [G]1 [H]5 [I]5 [L]1
[N]8 [O]8 [P]1 [R]3 [S]4 [T]7 [U]2 [V]1 [W]2 [Y]1
[A]1 [M]1 [N]2 [O]2 [S]1 [U]1 [Y]1 [—]1

PRAY AS IF EVERYTHING DEPENDED
ON GOD, AND WORK AS IF
EVERYTHING DEPENDED UPON MAN.
— FRANCIS CARDINAL SPELLMAN
[,]1 [.]1 [A]5 [D]8 [E]10 [F]2 [G]3 [H]2 [I]4 [K]1
[M]1 [N]8 [O]4 [P]4 [R]4 [S]2 [T]2 [U]1 [V]2 [W]1 [Y]3
[A]4 [C]2 [D]1 [E]1 [F]1 [I]2 [L]3 [M]1 [N]3 [P]1 [R]2 [S]2 [—]1

AN ATHEIST IS ONE WHO
HOPES THE LORD WILL DO
NOTHING TO DISTURB HIS
DISBELIEF. — FRANKLIN P. JONES
[.]1 [A]2 [B]2 [D]4 [E]6 [F]1 [G]1 [H]6 [I]8
[L]4 [N]4 [O]7 [P]1 [R]2 [S]6 [T]6 [U]1 [W]2
[.]1 [A]1 [E]1 [F]1 [I]1 [J]1 [K]1 [L]1 [N]3 [O]1 [P]1 [R]1 [S]1 [—]1

WE ARE NOT FREE TO USE
TODAY TO PROMISE TOMORROW
BECAUSE WE ARE ALREADY
MORTGAGED TO YESTERDAY.
— EMERSON
[.]1 [A]8 [B]1 [C]1 [D]4 [E]14 [F]1 [G]2 [I]1 [L]1
[M]3 [N]1 [O]10 [P]1 [R]9 [S]4 [T]8 [U]2 [W]3 [Y]4
[E]2 [M]1 [N]1 [O]1 [R]1 [S]1 [—]1

THE DESIRE FOR
IMAGINARY BENEFITS
OFTEN INVOLVES THE LOSS
OF PRESENT BLESSINGS.
— AESOP
[.]1 [A]2 [B]2 [D]1 [E]11 [F]4 [G]2 [H]2 [I]6
[L]3 [M]1 [N]6 [O]5 [P]1 [R]4 [S]9 [T]5 [V]2 [Y]1
[A]1 [E]1 [O]1 [P]1 [S]1 [—]1

**YOUR WILLINGNESS TO
WRESTLE WITH YOUR OWN
DEMONS WILL CAUSE
YOUR ANGELS TO SING.
— ANGUS WILSON**

[.]1 [A]2 [C]1 [D]1 [E]6 [G]3 [H]1 [I]5 [L]6
[M]1 [N]6 [O]7 [R]4 [S]7 [T]4 [U]4 [W]5 [Y]3
[A]1 [G]1 [I]1 [L]1 [N]2 [O]1 [S]2 [U]1 [W]1 [—]1

**TO BE AN ATHEIST REQUIRES AN
INFINITELY GREATER MEASURE OF
FAITH THAN TO RECEIVE ALL THE
GREAT TRUTHS WHICH ATHEISM
WOULD DENY. — JOSEPH ADDISON**

[.]1 [A]10 [B]1 [C]2 [D]2 [E]16 [F]3 [G]2 [H]8 [I]9 [L]4
[M]2 [N]6 [O]4 [Q]1 [R]8 [S]5 [T]13 [U]4 [V]1 [W]2 [Y]2
[A]1 [D]2 [E]1 [H]1 [I]1 [J]1 [N]1 [O]2 [P]1 [S]2 [—]1

**HERE'S A TEST TO FIND
OUT IF YOUR MISSION
ON EARTH IS FINISHED:
IF YOU'RE ALIVE, IT ISN'T.
— RICHARD BACH**

[']3 [,]1 [.]1 [:]1 [A]3 [D]2 [E]7 [F]4 [H]3 [I]11
[L]1 [M]1 [N]5 [O]6 [R]4 [S]7 [T]7 [U]3 [V]1 [Y]2
[A]2 [B]1 [C]2 [D]1 [H]2 [I]1 [R]2 [—]1

**WE SERVE BEST WHEN
WE REMEMBER THE
PURPOSE RATHER THAN
OUR PLACE IN THE
PROCESS. — ANONYMOUS**
    [.]1 [A]3 [B]2 [C]2 [E]15 [H]5 [I]1 [L]1 [M]2
    [N]3 [O]3 [P]4 [R]8 [S]5 [T]5 [U]2 [V]1 [W]3
    [A]1 [M]1 [N]2 [O]2 [S]1 [U]1 [Y]1 [—]1

**I ALWAYS PREFER TO
BELIEVE THE BEST OF
EVERYBODY. IT SAVES
SO MUCH TROUBLE.
— KIPLING**
    [.]2 [A]3 [B]4 [C]1 [D]1 [E]11 [F]2 [H]2 [I]3 [L]3
    [M]1 [O]5 [P]1 [R]4 [S]5 [T]5 [U]2 [V]3 [W]1 [Y]3
    [G]1 [I]2 [K]1 [L]1 [N]1 [P]1 [—]1

**KEEP YOUR HEART GOING
IN THE RIGHT DIRECTION,
AND YOU WON'T HAVE TO
WORRY ABOUT YOUR FEET.
— ANONYMOUS**
    [']1 [,]1 [.]1 [A]4 [B]1 [C]1 [D]2 [E]8 [F]1 [G]3 [H]4
    [I]5 [K]1 [N]5 [O]9 [P]1 [R]7 [T]8 [U]4 [V]1 [W]2 [Y]4
    [A]1 [M]1 [N]2 [O]2 [S]1 [U]1 [Y]1 [—]1

**MANY THINK THEY'RE
THINKING WHEN THEY'RE
MERELY REARRANGING
THEIR PREJUDICES.**
— REVISED WILLIAM JAMES

[']2 [.]1 [A]3 [C]1 [D]1 [E]11 [G]3 [H]6 [I]6 [J]1
[K]2 [L]1 [M]2 [N]7 [P]1 [R]8 [S]1 [T]5 [U]1 [W]1 [Y]4
[A]2 [D]1 [E]3 [I]3 [J]1 [L]2 [M]2 [R]1 [S]2 [V]1 [W]1 [—]1

**ABILITY MAY GET YOU
TO THE TOP, BUT IT
TAKES CHARACTER
TO KEEP YOU THERE.**
— JOHN WOODEN

[,]1 [.]1 [A]5 [B]2 [C]2 [E]8 [G]1 [H]3 [I]3
[K]2 [L]1 [M]1 [O]5 [P]2 [R]3 [S]1 [T]11 [U]3 [Y]4
[D]1 [E]1 [H]1 [J]1 [N]2 [O]3 [W]1 [—]1

**OPEN NOT THE DOOR TO A
LESSER EVIL, FOR
GREATER ONES INVARIABLY
SLINK IN AFTER IT.**
— REVISED BALTISAR GRACIÀN

[,]1 [.]1 [A]5 [B]1 [D]1 [E]9 [F]2 [G]1 [H]1 [I]6
[K]1 [L]4 [N]6 [O]7 [P]1 [R]7 [S]4 [T]6 [V]2 [Y]1
[A]4 [B]1 [C]1 [D]1 [E]2 [G]1 [I]3 [L]1 [N]1 [R]3 [S]2 [T]1 [V]1 [—]1

Faithfully Yours

The ABC's of belief

**FAITH SHOULDN'T BE
SHAKEN, BUT STIRRED.**
[']1 [,]1 [.]1 [A]2 [B]2 [D]2 [E]3 [F]1 [H]3
[I]2 [K]1 [L]1 [N]2 [O]1 [R]2 [S]3 [T]4 [U]2

**FAITH IS THE SUBSTANCE
OF THINGS HOPED FOR.
— HEBREWS 11:1**
[—]1 [.]1 [1]3 [:]1 [A]2 [B]2 [C]1 [D]1 [E]5 [F]3
[G]1 [H]5 [I]3 [N]2 [O]3 [P]1 [R]2 [S]5 [T]4 [U]1 [W]1

**HERE, BELIEVE.
THERE, UNDERSTAND.**
(*Wings of Silver*)
[,]2 [.]2 [A]1 [B]1 [D]2 [E]8 [H]2
[I]1 [L]1 [N]2 [R]3 [S]1 [T]2 [U]1 [V]1

**OURS IS A CAN-DO
KIND OF FAITH — WE
CAN DO ALL THINGS
THROUGH CHRIST.**
[-]1 [—]1 [.]1 [A]5 [C]3 [D]3 [E]1 [F]2 [G]2 [H]5
[I]5 [K]1 [L]2 [N]4 [O]5 [R]3 [S]4 [T]4 [U]2 [W]1

**YES, VIRGINIA,
THERE IS A SAVIOR.**
[,]2 [.]1 [A]3 [E]3 [G]1 [H]1 [I]5
[N]1 [O]1 [R]3 [S]3 [T]1 [V]2 [Y]1

**FAITH GROWS
IN THE VALLEY.**
(*Wings of Silver*)
[.]1 [A]2 [E]2 [F]1 [G]1 [H]2 [I]2 [L]2
[N]1 [O]1 [R]1 [S]1 [T]2 [V]1 [W]1 [Y]1

**DOUBT IS OFTEN
THE COMPANION
OF FAITH.**
[.]1 [A]2 [B]1 [C]1 [D]1 [E]2 [F]3 [H]2
[I]3 [M]1 [N]3 [O]5 [P]1 [S]1 [T]4 [U]1

**FAITH
DOESN'T FALL APART
AT THE SEEMS.**
[']1 [.]1 [A]5 [D]1 [E]4 [F]2 [H]2 [I]1
[L]2 [M]1 [N]1 [O]1 [P]1 [R]1 [S]3 [T]5

**WITHOUT FAITH, WE ARE
AS STAINED GLASS
WINDOWS IN THE DARK.
— ANONYMOUS**
[,]1 [.]1 [A]6 [D]3 [E]4 [F]1 [G]1 [H]3 [I]5
[K]1 [L]1 [N]3 [O]2 [R]2 [S]5 [T]5 [U]1 [W]4
[A]1 [M]1 [N]2 [O]2 [S]1 [U]1 [Y]1 [—]1

**IT'S NOT ENOUGH
TO BE DEFENDERS
OF THE FAITH.**
[']1 [.]1 [A]1 [B]1 [D]2 [E]6 [F]3 [G]1
[H]3 [I]2 [N]3 [O]4 [R]1 [S]2 [T]5 [U]1

GRAY AREAS
USUALLY BEGIN
IN GRAY MATTER.
[.]1 [A]6 [B]1 [E]3 [G]3 [I]2 [L]2
[M]1 [N]2 [R]4 [S]2 [T]2 [U]2 [Y]3

IT'S HARD TO BE AN
ATHEIST WHEN THERE'S
SO MUCH AROUND US
TO BELIEVE IN.
[']2 [.]1 [A]4 [B]2 [C]1 [D]2 [E]8 [H]5 [I]4
[L]1 [M]1 [N]4 [O]4 [R]3 [S]5 [T]6 [U]3 [V]1 [W]1

RELIGION ISN'T
THE ANSWER.
[']1 [.]1 [A]1 [E]3 [G]1 [H]1 [I]3
[L]1 [N]3 [O]1 [R]2 [S]2 [T]2 [W]1

IF YOUR FAITH FEELS
A LITTLE FLIGHTY,
GET GROUNDED
IN THE WORD.
[,]1 [.]1 [A]2 [D]3 [E]6 [F]4 [G]3 [H]3 [I]5
[L]4 [N]2 [O]3 [R]3 [S]1 [T]6 [U]2 [W]1 [Y]2

DOUBT IS A PAIN
TOO LONELY TO KNOW
THAT FAITH IS HIS TWIN
BROTHER. — KAHLIL GIBRAN
[.]1 [A]4 [B]2 [D]1 [E]2 [F]1 [H]4 [I]6 [K]1
[L]2 [N]4 [O]7 [P]1 [R]2 [S]3 [T]8 [U]1 [W]2 [Y]1
[A]2 [B]1 [G]1 [H]1 [I]2 [K]1 [L]1 [N]1 [R]1 [—]1

IT'S NOT DYING FOR
FAITH THAT'S SO
HARD. IT'S LIVING UP
TO IT. — W. M. THACKERY
[']3 [.]2 [A]3 [D]2 [F]2 [G]2 [H]3 [I]7 [L]1
[N]3 [O]4 [P]1 [R]2 [S]4 [T]8 [U]1 [V]1 [Y]1
[.]2 [A]1 [C]1 [E]1 [H]1 [K]1 [M]1 [R]1 [T]1 [W]1 [Y]1 [—]1

DON'T BELIEVE IN GOD?
HE BELIEVES IN YOU.
[']1 [.]1 [?]1 [B]2 [D]2 [E]7 [G]1 [H]1
[I]4 [L]2 [N]3 [O]3 [S]1 [T]1 [U]1 [V]2 [Y]1

FAITH
UNDER
CONSTRUCTION.
[.]1 [A]1 [C]2 [D]1 [E]1 [F]1 [H]1
[I]2 [N]3 [O]2 [R]2 [S]1 [T]3 [U]2

IF WE STAND,
HE'LL DELIVER.
[']1 [,]1 [.]1 [A]1 [D]2 [E]4 [F]1 [H]1
[I]2 [L]3 [N]1 [R]1 [S]1 [T]1 [V]1 [W]1

WHAT WAS SPOKEN
TO US IN THE LIGHT
WILL BE TESTED
IN THE DARKNESS.
[.]1 [A]3 [B]1 [D]2 [E]7 [G]1 [H]4 [I]4 [K]2
[L]3 [N]4 [O]2 [P]1 [R]1 [S]6 [T]7 [U]1 [W]3

**SOMETIMES WE HAVE
TO TAKE GOD
AT FAITH VALUE.**

[.]1 [A]5 [D]1 [E]6 [F]1 [G]1 [H]2 [I]2
[K]1 [L]1 [M]2 [O]3 [S]2 [T]5 [U]1 [V]2 [W]1

**DON'T MAKE UP YOUR
MIND BEFORE YOU'VE
LISTENED TO YOUR HEART.**

[']2 [.]1 [A]2 [B]1 [D]3 [E]7 [F]1 [H]1 [I]2 [K]1
[L]1 [M]2 [N]3 [O]6 [P]1 [R]4 [S]1 [T]4 [U]4 [V]1 [Y]3

KEEP THE FAITH.

[.]1 [A]1 [E]3 [F]1 [H]2
[I]1 [K]1 [P]1 [T]2

**WHEN TROUBLE MAKES
IT HARD TO SMILE,
PUT ON A BRAVE FAITH.**

[,]1 [.]1 [A]5 [B]2 [D]1 [E]5 [F]1 [H]3 [I]3 [K]1
[L]2 [M]2 [N]2 [O]3 [P]1 [R]3 [S]2 [T]5 [U]2 [V]1 [W]1

**TO TAKE GOD'S HAND
IS TO LET GO
OF ALL ELSE.
— ANONYMOUS**

[']1 [.]1 [A]3 [D]2 [E]4 [F]1 [G]2
[H]1 [I]1 [K]1 [L]4 [N]1 [O]5 [S]3 [T]4
[A]1 [M]1 [N]2 [O]2 [S]1 [U]1 [Y]1 [—]1

AN ACT OF FAITH
PROBABLY SHOULDN'T
EXPECT APPLAUSE.
[']1 [.]1 [A]6 [B]2 [C]2 [D]1 [E]3 [F]2 [H]2 [I]1
[L]3 [N]2 [O]3 [P]4 [R]1 [S]2 [T]4 [U]2 [X]1 [Y]1

THE HEART'S GRASP
EXCEEDS THE
MIND'S REACH.
[']2 [.]1 [A]3 [C]2 [D]2 [E]7 [G]1 [H]4
[I]1 [M]1 [N]1 [P]1 [R]3 [S]4 [T]3 [X]1

BEGIN TO WEAVE,
AND GOD WILL GIVE
YOU THE THREAD.
— GERMAN PROVERB
[,]1 [.]1 [A]3 [B]1 [D]3 [E]6 [G]3 [H]2 [I]3
[L]2 [N]2 [O]3 [R]1 [T]3 [U]1 [V]2 [W]2 [Y]1
[A]1 [B]1 [E]2 [G]1 [M]1 [N]1 [O]1 [P]1 [R]3 [V]1 [—]1

BELIEVE IN SOMETHING
OR YOU'LL FALL
FOR ANYTHING.
[']1 [.]1 [A]2 [B]1 [E]4 [F]2 [G]2 [H]2 [I]4
[L]5 [M]1 [N]4 [O]4 [R]2 [S]1 [T]2 [U]1 [V]1 [Y]2

A LESSON LEARNED
BY HEART OFTEN
BOGGLES THE MIND.
[.]1 [A]3 [B]2 [D]2 [E]7 [F]1 [G]2 [H]2
[I]1 [L]3 [M]1 [N]4 [O]3 [R]2 [S]3 [T]3 [Y]1

Can I Get A Witness?

Examining our example in light of his

FIRST WE REACH UP,
THEN WE CAN
REACH OUT.
[,]1 [.]1 [A]3 [C]3 [E]5 [F]1 [H]3 [I]1
[N]2 [O]1 [P]1 [R]3 [S]1 [T]3 [U]2 [W]2

LIVE SO THAT THOSE
WHO KNOW YOU WILL
COME TO KNOW GOD.
[.]1 [A]1 [C]1 [D]1 [E]3 [G]1 [H]3 [I]2 [K]2
[L]3 [M]1 [N]2 [O]9 [S]2 [T]4 [U]1 [V]1 [W]4 [Y]1

WILL YOU BE
THE ONE TO STAND
WHEN OTHERS FALL?
[?]1 [A]2 [B]1 [D]1 [E]5 [F]1 [H]3 [I]1
[L]4 [N]3 [O]4 [R]1 [S]2 [T]4 [U]1 [W]2 [Y]1

EVERY LIFE TELLS A
STORY. ARE YOU GOING
FOR INSPIRATIONAL
OR HORROR?
[.]1 [?]1 [A]4 [E]5 [F]2 [G]2 [H]1 [I]5 [L]4
[N]3 [O]8 [P]1 [R]9 [S]3 [T]3 [U]1 [V]1 [Y]3

49

**EVERYONE HAS
AT LEAST ONE SERMON
IN HIM. — ANONYMOUS**
[.]1 [A]3 [E]6 [H]2 [I]2 [L]1 [M]2
[N]4 [O]3 [R]2 [S]3 [T]2 [V]1 [Y]1
[A]1 [M]1 [N]2 [O]2 [S]1 [U]1 [Y]1 [—]1

**PEOPLE TO SEE.
THINGS TO DO.
A WORLD TO RESCUE.**
[.]3 [A]1 [C]1 [D]2 [E]6 [G]1 [H]1 [I]1
[L]2 [N]1 [O]6 [P]2 [R]2 [S]3 [T]4 [U]1 [W]1

**MEMORIZE SCRIPTURE,
AND WHEN IT'S NEEDED,
YOU CAN JUST
SAY THE WORD.**
[']1 [,]2 [.]1 [A]3 [C]2 [D]4 [E]8 [H]2 [I]3 [J]1
[M]2 [N]4 [O]3 [P]1 [R]4 [S]4 [T]4 [U]3 [W]2 [Y]2 [Z]1

**THE NEXT TIME
SOMEONE ASKS,
JUST SAY THE WORD.**
[,]1 [.]1 [A]2 [D]1 [E]6 [H]2 [I]1 [J]1 [K]1
[M]2 [N]2 [O]3 [R]1 [S]5 [T]5 [U]1 [W]1 [X]1 [Y]1

**AFTER ALL'S SAID AND
DONE, WHAT COUNTS IS
NOT WHAT WE'VE SAID
BUT DONE.**
[']2 [,]1 [.]1 [A]7 [B]1 [C]1 [D]5 [E]5 [F]1 [H]2
[I]3 [L]2 [N]5 [O]4 [R]1 [S]5 [T]6 [U]2 [V]1 [W]3

YOU MAY HAVE TO GO
OUT OF YOUR WAY TO
SHOW SOMEONE THE WAY.
[.]1 [A]4 [E]4 [F]1 [G]1 [H]3 [M]2 [N]1
[O]10 [R]1 [S]2 [T]4 [U]3 [V]1 [W]3 [Y]5

IS GOD'S ARMY
ON ACTIVE DUTY?
[']1 [?]1 [A]2 [C]1 [D]2 [E]1 [G]1 [I]2
[M]1 [N]1 [O]2 [R]1 [S]2 [T]2 [U]1 [V]1 [Y]2

GOD CALLS US TO BE
FISHERS OF MEN, BUT
SOME OF US HAVE
OTHER FISH TO FRY.
[,]1 [.]1 [A]2 [B]2 [C]1 [D]1 [E]6 [F]5 [G]1 [H]4
[I]2 [L]2 [M]2 [N]1 [O]7 [R]3 [S]7 [T]4 [U]3 [V]1 [Y]1

LEAVE YOUR MARK,
NOT A STAIN.
[,]1 [.]1 [A]4 [E]2 [I]1 [K]1 [L]1 [M]1
[N]2 [O]2 [R]2 [S]1 [T]2 [U]1 [V]1 [Y]1

SOMETIMES WHAT WE ARE
THUNDERS SO LOUD
NO ONE CAN HEAR
WHAT WE SAY.
(*Wings of Silver*)
[.]1 [A]6 [C]1 [D]2 [E]8 [H]4 [I]1 [L]1
[M]2 [N]4 [O]5 [R]3 [S]5 [T]4 [U]2 [W]4 [Y]1

**CAN YOUR CREED
BE RECOGNIZED
IN YOUR DEED?**
(*Wings of Silver*)
[?]1 [A]1 [B]1 [C]3 [D]4 [E]7 [G]1
[I]2 [N]3 [O]3 [R]4 [U]2 [Y]2 [Z]1

**YOU MAY BE THE
ONLY BIBLE SOME
PEOPLE EVER READ.**
(*Wings of Silver*)
[.]1 [A]2 [B]3 [D]1 [E]9 [H]1 [I]1 [L]3 [M]2
[N]1 [O]4 [P]2 [R]2 [S]1 [T]1 [U]1 [V]1 [Y]3

**YOU TOO HAVE
A MARQUEE.
IT'S YOUR LIFE.**
[']1 [.]2 [A]3 [E]4 [F]1 [H]1 [I]2 [L]1
[M]1 [O]4 [Q]1 [R]2 [S]1 [T]2 [U]3 [V]1 [Y]2

**THE SECRET
TO REACHING
ISN'T ALWAYS
PREACHING.**
[']1 [.]1 [A]4 [C]3 [E]5 [G]2 [H]3 [I]3
[L]1 [N]3 [O]1 [P]1 [R]3 [S]3 [T]4 [W]1 [Y]1

**IF SOMEONE YOU KNOW
IS PLAYING WITH FIRE,
IT'S OKAY TO BE
A WET BLANKET.**
[']1 [,]1 [.]1 [A]4 [B]2 [E]6 [F]2 [G]1 [H]1 [I]6 [K]3
[L]2 [M]1 [N]4 [O]6 [P]1 [R]1 [S]3 [T]5 [U]1 [W]3 [Y]3

MAY OTHERS SEE
THE BEAUTY OF
JESUS IN YOU.
[.]1 [A]2 [B]1 [E]6 [F]1 [H]2 [I]1 [J]1
[M]1 [N]1 [O]3 [R]1 [S]4 [T]3 [U]3 [Y]3

SEE THE MJESUSE.
— ANONYMOUS
[.]1 [E]5 [H]1 [J]1 [M]1 [S]3 [T]1 [U]1
[A]1 [M]1 [N]2 [O]2 [S]1 [U]1 [Y]1 [—]1

SHARE JESUS
AND YOU DIVVY
UP THE DEVIL.
[.]1 [A]2 [D]3 [E]4 [H]2 [I]2 [J]1 [L]1
[N]1 [O]1 [P]1 [R]1 [S]3 [T]1 [U]3 [V]3 [Y]2

RANSOM THE PLANET.
[.]1 [A]2 [E]2 [H]1 [L]1 [M]1
[N]2 [O]1 [P]1 [R]1 [S]1 [T]2

GOD SENT
A REPAIR CREW FOR
THIS BROKEN WORLD
— AND WE'RE IT.
[']1 [—]1 [.]1 [A]3 [B]1 [C]1 [D]3 [E]6 [F]1 [G]1
[H]1 [I]3 [K]1 [L]1 [N]3 [O]4 [P]1 [R]7 [S]2 [T]3 [W]3

NO FEAR.
— PHILEMON 1:14
[—]1 [.]1 [1]2 [4]1 [:]1 [A]1 [E]2 [F]1
[H]1 [I]1 [L]1 [M]1 [N]2 [O]2 [P]1 [R]1

GONE FISHING.
— MATTHEW 4:19, 20
[,]1 [—]1 [.]1 [0]1 [1]1 [2]1 [4]1 [9]1 [:]1 [A]1
[E]2 [F]1 [G]2 [H]2 [I]2 [M]1 [N]2 [O]1 [S]1 [T]2 [W]1

LOVE 'EM —
THAT'LL TEACH 'EM.
[']3 [—]1 [.]1 [A]2 [C]1 [E]4 [H]2 [L]3 [M]2 [O]1 [T]3 [V]1

God The Father

He is Elohim, Yahweh, Jehovah, and Adonai,
but he's always Dad to you

YOU CAN READ
GOD LIKE A BOOK.
    [.]1 [A]3 [B]1 [C]1 [D]2 [E]2 [G]1
    [I]1 [K]2 [L]1 [N]1 [O]4 [R]1 [U]1 [Y]1

THE ONE THING GOD
DOESN'T KNOW: A SOUL
HE DOESN'T LOVE.
— LARRY ALLGOOD
    [']2 [.]1 [:]1 [A]1 [D]3 [E]6 [G]2 [H]3 [I]1
    [K]1 [L]2 [N]5 [O]7 [S]3 [T]4 [U]1 [V]1 [W]1
    [A]2 [D]1 [G]1 [L]3 [O]2 [R]2 [Y]1 [—]1

GIVE HIM ALL HONOR,
HIS PEOPLE ON EARTH.
    [,]1 [.]1 [A]2 [E]4 [G]1 [H]4 [I]3 [L]3
    [M]1 [N]2 [O]4 [P]2 [R]2 [S]1 [T]1 [V]1

MOST OF OUR QUESTIONS
COME DOWN TO JUST
ONE: HOW MUCH DO WE
TRUST THE FATHER?
    [:]1 [?]1 [A]1 [C]2 [D]2 [E]6 [F]2 [H]4 [I]1
    [J]1 [M]3 [N]3 [O]10 [Q]1 [R]3 [S]5 [T]8 [U]5 [W]3

**GOD DOESN'T
LAY DOWN THE LAW.
HE WRITES IT
ON OUR HEARTS.**
[']1 [.]2 [A]3 [D]3 [E]5 [G]1 [H]3 [I]2
[L]2 [N]3 [O]5 [R]3 [S]3 [T]5 [U]1 [W]3 [Y]1

**FOR GOD SO LOVED
THE WORLD ...
BOY, DO WE LOVE
SAYING THAT.**
[,]1 [.]4 [A]2 [B]1 [D]4 [E]4 [F]1 [G]2 [H]2
[I]1 [L]3 [N]1 [O]8 [R]2 [S]2 [T]3 [V]2 [W]2 [Y]2

**IN THE DARK ABOUT
SOMETHING? WE KNOW
A NEVER-ENDING
LIGHT SUPPLY.**
[-]1 [.]1 [?]1 [A]3 [B]1 [D]2 [E]6 [G]3 [H]3 [I]4 [K]2
[L]2 [M]1 [N]6 [O]3 [P]2 [R]2 [S]2 [T]4 [U]2 [V]1 [W]2 [Y]1

**PRAISE IS A RESPONSE
TO GOD'S LOVE. WORSHIP
IS A RESPONSE TO
HIS RIGHTEOUSNESS.**
[']1 [.]2 [A]3 [D]1 [E]8 [G]2 [H]3 [I]6 [L]1
[N]3 [O]8 [P]4 [R]5 [S]13 [T]3 [U]1 [V]1 [W]1

**GUILT COMES FROM
SOMEWHERE. GRACE
COMES OUT OF NOWHERE.**
[.]2 [A]1 [C]3 [E]8 [F]2 [G]2 [H]2 [I]1
[L]1 [M]4 [N]1 [O]7 [R]4 [S]3 [T]2 [U]2 [W]2

YOU'RE ONE OF THE
BEST THINGS
HE EVER MADE.

[']1 [.]1 [A]1 [B]1 [D]1 [E]8 [F]1 [G]1 [H]3
[I]1 [M]1 [N]2 [O]3 [R]2 [S]2 [T]3 [U]1 [V]1 [Y]1

IT'S NOT SO MUCH
WHERE BUT WHO
YOU WORSHIP.

[']1 [.]1 [B]1 [C]1 [E]2 [H]4 [I]2 [M]1
[N]1 [O]5 [P]1 [R]2 [S]3 [T]3 [U]3 [W]3 [Y]1

HE IS NOT A GOD
OF THE DEAD,
BUT OF THE LIVING.
— LUKE 20:38

[,]1 [—]1 [.]1 [0]1 [2]1 [3]1 [8]1 [:]1 [A]2 [B]1 [D]3 [E]5
[F]2 [G]2 [H]3 [I]3 [K]1 [L]2 [N]2 [O]4 [S]1 [T]4 [U]2 [V]1

DOES GOD HAVE A SENSE
OF HUMOR? LOOK AT
YOUR HAIR IN THE
MORNING, THEN DECIDE.

[,]1 [.]1 [?]1 [A]4 [C]1 [D]4 [E]8 [F]1 [G]2 [H]5 [I]4
[K]1 [L]1 [M]2 [N]5 [O]8 [R]4 [S]3 [T]3 [U]2 [V]1 [Y]1

GOD ENTERS BY A
PRIVATE DOOR INTO
EVERY INDIVIDUAL.
— EMERSON

[.]1 [A]3 [B]1 [D]4 [E]5 [G]1 [I]5 [L]1
[N]3 [O]4 [P]1 [R]4 [S]1 [T]3 [U]1 [V]3 [Y]2
[E]2 [M]1 [N]1 [O]1 [R]1 [S]1 [—]1

GOD BLESS
US EVERY ONE.
— DICKENS
    [.]1 [B]1 [D]1 [E]4 [G]1 [L]1
    [N]1 [O]2 [R]1 [S]3 [U]1 [V]1 [Y]1
    [C]1 [D]1 [E]1 [I]1 [K]1 [N]1 [S]1 [—]1

THE BROTHERS
SAY WE'RE ON A
MISSION FROM GOD.
    [']1 [.]1 [A]2 [B]1 [D]1 [E]4 [F]1 [G]1 [H]2
    [I]2 [M]2 [N]2 [O]5 [R]4 [S]4 [T]2 [W]1 [Y]1

EVEN IF TIME
ISN'T ON YOUR
SIDE, THE FATHER IS.
    [']1 [,]1 [.]1 [A]1 [D]1 [E]6 [F]2 [H]2 [I]5
    [M]1 [N]3 [O]2 [R]2 [S]3 [T]4 [U]1 [V]1 [Y]1

IF GOD HAD A DESK,
HE'D NEVER BE
AWAY FROM IT.
    [']1 [,]1 [.]1 [A]4 [B]1 [D]4 [E]5 [F]2 [G]1 [H]2
    [I]2 [K]1 [M]1 [N]1 [O]2 [R]2 [S]1 [T]1 [V]1 [W]1 [Y]1

OUR GOD IS AN
AWESOME GOD.
    [.]1 [A]2 [D]2 [E]2 [G]2 [I]1
    [M]1 [N]1 [O]4 [R]1 [S]2 [U]1 [W]1

TO KNOW HIM IS
TO LOVE HIM.
[.]1 [E]1 [H]2 [I]3 [K]1 [L]1
[M]2 [N]1 [O]4 [S]1 [T]2 [V]1 [W]1

YOU'RE SMART ENOUGH,
YOU'RE GOOD ENOUGH,
— AND DOGGONE IT,
GOD LOVES YOU.
[']2 [,]3 [—]1 [.]1 [A]2 [D]4 [E]6 [G]6 [H]2 [I]1
[L]1 [M]1 [N]4 [O]11 [R]3 [S]2 [T]2 [U]5 [V]1 [Y]3

GOD DOESN'T HAVE TO
SEE INTO THE FUTURE—
HE'S ALREADY THERE.
[']2 [—]1 [.]1 [A]3 [D]3 [E]10 [F]1 [G]1 [H]4
[I]1 [L]1 [N]2 [O]4 [R]3 [S]3 [T]6 [U]2 [V]1 [Y]1

LET THE PEOPLE
BE GLAD THAT
OUR GOD REIGNS.
[.]1 [A]2 [B]1 [D]2 [E]6 [G]3 [H]2 [I]1
[L]3 [N]1 [O]3 [P]2 [R]2 [S]1 [T]4 [U]1

HE ALWAYS WANTS TO
GIVE US ANOTHER
CHANCE TO GET IT
RIGHT THIS TIME.
[.]1 [A]5 [C]2 [E]6 [G]3 [H]5 [I]5 [L]1 [M]1
[N]3 [O]3 [R]2 [S]4 [T]9 [U]1 [V]1 [W]2 [Y]1

**GOD'S WAYS
ARE WONDROUS.**
[']1 [.]1 [A]2 [D]2 [E]1 [G]1
[N]1 [O]3 [R]2 [S]3 [U]1 [W]2 [Y]1

**ORANGE YOU GLAD
YOU'RE THE APPLE
OF HIS EYE?**
[']1 [?]1 [A]3 [D]1 [E]6 [F]1 [G]2 [H]2 [I]1
[L]2 [N]1 [O]4 [P]2 [R]2 [S]1 [T]1 [U]2 [Y]3

**GOD HAS NO
GRANDCHILDREN,
ONLY CHILDREN.**
[,]1 [.]1 [A]2 [C]2 [D]4 [E]2 [G]2
[H]3 [I]2 [L]3 [N]5 [O]3 [R]3 [S]1 [Y]1

**IT CAN BE LONELY
AT THE TOP.
THAT'S WHY GOD
MADE US.**
[']1 [.]2 [A]4 [B]1 [C]1 [D]2 [E]4 [G]1 [H]3 [I]1
[L]2 [M]1 [N]2 [O]3 [P]1 [S]2 [T]6 [U]1 [W]1 [Y]2

**TONIGHT'S PICK THREE:
THE FATHER, THE SON,
AND THE HOLY GHOST.**
[']1 [,]2 [.]1 [:]1 [A]2 [C]1 [D]1 [E]6 [F]1 [G]2
[H]8 [I]2 [K]1 [L]1 [N]3 [O]4 [P]1 [R]2 [S]3 [T]8 [Y]1

YOU DON'T HAVE TO GO
THROUGH CHANNELS
TO GET TO GOD.
   [']1 [.]1 [A]2 [C]1 [D]2 [E]3 [G]4 [H]4
   [L]1 [N]3 [O]8 [R]1 [S]1 [T]6 [U]2 [V]1 [Y]1

MIND YOUR FATHER.
   [.]1 [A]1 [D]1 [E]1 [F]1 [H]1 [I]1
   [M]1 [N]1 [O]1 [R]2 [T]1 [U]1 [Y]1

LIFE IS WORTH LIVING.
PEOPLE ARE
WORTH LOVING.
GOD IS WORTH TRUSTING.
   [.]3 [A]1 [D]1 [E]4 [F]1 [G]4 [H]3 [I]7 [L]4
   [N]3 [O]6 [P]2 [R]5 [S]3 [T]5 [U]1 [V]2 [W]3

HE CALLS THE TUNE,
AND IT'S
"BLESSED ASSURANCE."
   ["]1 ["]1 [']1 [,]1 [.]1 [A]4 [B]1 [C]2 [D]2
   [E]6 [H]2 [I]1 [L]3 [N]3 [R]1 [S]6 [T]3 [U]2

ALL MY CHILDREN,
I'M THE GUIDING LIGHT
TO THE YOUNG AND
THE RESTLESS.
   [']1 [,]1 [.]1 [A]2 [C]1 [D]3 [E]6 [G]4 [H]5
   [I]5 [L]5 [M]2 [N]4 [O]2 [R]2 [S]3 [T]6 [U]2 [Y]2

God The Son

Getting to know the brother
with whom we've all got blood ties

THE SAVIOR
ACED HIS SERVE.
[.]1 [A]2 [C]1 [D]1 [E]4 [H]2 [I]2 [O]1 [R]2 [S]3 [T]1 [V]2

JESUS SAID HIS PEACE.
[.]1 [A]2 [C]1 [D]1 [E]3 [H]1 [I]2 [J]1 [P]1 [S]4 [U]1

JESUS CHRIST —
THE SAME YESTERDAY,
AND TODAY, AND FOREVER!
— HEBREWS 13:8
[!]1 [,]2 [—]2 [1]1 [3]1 [8]1 [:]1 [A]5 [B]1 [C]1 [D]4 [E]9 [F]1
[H]3 [I]1 [J]1 [M]1 [N]2 [O]2 [R]5 [S]6 [T]4 [U]1 [V]1 [W]1 [Y]3

JESUS!
LIVE AND IN PERSONS!
[!]2 [A]1 [D]1 [E]3 [I]2 [J]1 [L]1
[N]3 [O]1 [P]1 [R]1 [S]4 [U]1 [V]1

WHO SHALL SEPARATE
US FROM THE LOVE
OF CHRIST?
— ROMANS 8:35
[—]1 [3]1 [5]1 [8]1 [:]1 [?]1 [A]4 [C]1 [E]4 [F]2 [H]4
[I]1 [L]3 [M]2 [N]1 [O]5 [P]1 [R]4 [S]5 [T]3 [U]1 [V]1 [W]1

LET'S GIVE IT UP
FOR THE KING
OF HEART AND SOUL.
  [']1 [.]1 [A]2 [D]1 [E]4 [F]2 [G]2 [H]2 [I]3
  [K]1 [L]2 [N]2 [O]3 [P]1 [R]2 [S]2 [T]4 [U]2 [V]1

SON WORSHIPPERS
LOOK RADIANT.
  [.]1 [A]2 [D]1 [E]1 [H]1 [I]2 [K]1
  [L]1 [N]2 [O]4 [P]2 [R]3 [S]3 [T]1 [W]1

CHRIST'S KINGDOM IS
HEAVEN ON EARTH.
  [']1 [.]1 [A]2 [C]1 [D]1 [E]3 [G]1 [H]3
  [I]3 [K]1 [M]1 [N]3 [O]2 [R]2 [S]3 [T]2 [V]1

IF GOD WERE ONE
OF US, HIS NAME
WOULD BE JESUS.
  [,]1 [.]1 [A]1 [B]1 [D]2 [E]6 [F]2 [G]1 [H]1
  [I]2 [J]1 [L]1 [M]1 [N]2 [O]4 [R]1 [S]4 [U]3 [W]2

TIME FLIES
WHEN YOU'RE
FOLLOWING THE SON.
  [']1 [.]1 [E]5 [F]2 [G]1 [H]2 [I]3 [L]3
  [M]1 [N]3 [O]4 [R]1 [S]2 [T]2 [U]1 [W]2 [Y]1

TODAY'S YOUR LUCKY
DAY — JESUS LOVES YOU!
  [!]1 [']1 [—]1 [A]2 [C]1 [D]2 [E]2 [J]1
  [K]1 [L]2 [O]4 [R]1 [S]4 [T]1 [U]4 [V]1 [Y]5

SPIRITS AND
EYEBROWS:
JESUS RAISED
THEM BOTH.
[.]1 [:]1 [A]2 [B]2 [D]2 [E]5 [H]2 [I]3 [J]1
[M]1 [N]1 [O]2 [P]1 [R]3 [S]6 [T]3 [U]1 [W]1 [Y]1

DIDN'T MARY'S BOY
TURN OUT WELL?
[']2 [?]1 [A]1 [B]1 [D]2 [E]1 [I]1 [L]2
[M]1 [N]2 [O]2 [R]2 [S]1 [T]3 [U]2 [W]1 [Y]2

JESUS. HE MEETS
YOUR MINIMUM
DAILY REQUIREMENTS.
[.]2 [A]1 [D]1 [E]7 [H]1 [I]4 [J]1 [L]1
[M]5 [N]2 [O]1 [Q]1 [R]3 [S]4 [T]2 [U]4 [Y]2

JESUS IS
AN OPEN BOOK.
[.]1 [A]1 [B]1 [E]2 [I]1 [J]1 [K]1 [N]2 [O]3 [P]1 [S]3 [U]1

UNDER THE
SAME MANAGEMENT
FOR 2,000 YEARS.
— ANONYMOUS
[,]1 [.]1 [0]3 [2]1 [A]4 [D]1 [E]6 [F]1 [G]1
[H]1 [M]3 [N]3 [O]1 [R]3 [S]2 [T]2 [U]1 [Y]1
[A]1 [M]1 [N]2 [O]2 [S]1 [U]1 [Y]1 [—]1

Growing Up To Be Like Him

Making a case for coming of age in Christ

**GROWTH IS THE
ONLY EVIDENCE
OF LIFE.**
— JOHN HENRY NEWMAN
　[.]1 [C]1 [D]1 [E]5 [F]2 [G]1 [H]2 [I]3
　[L]2 [N]2 [O]3 [R]1 [S]1 [T]2 [V]1 [W]1 [Y]1
　[A]1 [E]2 [H]2 [J]1 [M]1 [N]4 [O]1 [R]1 [W]1 [Y]1 [—]1

**ARE YOU ON A
SPIRITUAL JOURNEY
OR GURNEY?**
　[?]1 [A]3 [E]3 [G]1 [I]2 [J]1 [L]1
　[N]3 [O]4 [P]1 [R]5 [S]1 [T]1 [U]4 [Y]3

**WHAT OTHERS THINK OF
YOU HAS NO BEARING ON
WHAT GOD WANTS YOU TO
BE. — GLENDA DRAKE**
　[.]1 [A]5 [B]2 [D]1 [E]3 [F]1 [G]2 [H]5 [I]2
　[K]1 [N]5 [O]8 [R]2 [S]3 [T]6 [U]2 [W]3 [Y]2
　[A]2 [D]2 [E]2 [G]1 [K]1 [L]1 [N]1 [R]1 [—]1

**THIS IS MATURITY:
TO DO ONE'S DUTY
WITHOUT BEING
SUPERVISED.**
(*Wings of Silver*)
　[']1 [.]1 [:]1 [A]1 [B]1 [D]3 [E]4 [G]1 [H]2 [I]6
　[M]1 [N]2 [O]4 [P]1 [R]2 [S]5 [T]7 [U]4 [V]1 [W]1 [Y]2

WHEN YOU GIVE TO GOD,
YOU ALWAYS
GET BACK CHANGE.

[,]1 [.]1 [A]4 [B]1 [C]2 [D]1 [E]4 [G]4 [H]2 [I]1
[K]1 [L]1 [N]2 [O]4 [S]1 [T]2 [U]2 [V]1 [W]2 [Y]3

DO YOU TAKE AFTER
YOUR FATHER?

[?]1 [A]3 [D]1 [E]3 [F]2 [H]1
[K]1 [O]3 [R]3 [T]3 [U]2 [Y]2

REMEMBER WHEN
CHRISTIAN
MEANT
CHRIST-LIKE?

[-]1 [?]1 [A]2 [B]1 [C]2 [E]6 [H]3 [I]4
[K]1 [L]1 [M]3 [N]3 [R]4 [S]2 [T]3 [W]1

MATURITY IS
PRODUCING MORE
THAN YOU CONSUME.
— ANONYMOUS

[.]1 [A]2 [C]2 [D]1 [E]2 [G]1 [H]1 [I]3
[M]3 [N]3 [O]4 [P]1 [R]3 [S]2 [T]3 [U]4 [Y]2
[A]1 [M]1 [N]2 [O]2 [S]1 [U]1 [Y]1 [—]1

ALL HE ASKS IS
ALL YOU'VE GOT.

[']1 [.]1 [A]3 [E]2 [G]1 [H]1 [I]1
[K]1 [L]4 [O]2 [S]3 [T]1 [U]1 [V]1 [Y]1

**CHRISTIANS GROW IN
LEAPS AND REBOUNDS.**
[.]1 [A]3 [B]1 [C]1 [D]2 [E]2 [G]1 [H]1 [I]3
[L]1 [N]4 [O]2 [P]1 [R]3 [S]4 [T]1 [U]1 [W]1

**WHEN YOU THROW DIRT,
YOU LOSE GROUND.
— TEXAS PROVERB**
[,]1 [.]1 [D]2 [E]2 [G]1 [H]2 [I]1 [L]1
[N]2 [O]5 [R]3 [S]1 [T]2 [U]3 [W]2 [Y]2
[A]1 [B]1 [E]2 [N]1 [O]1 [P]1 [R]2 [T]1 [V]1 [X]1 [—]1

**CONFESSED FAULTS
ARE HALF MENDED.
— SCOTTISH PROVERB**
[.]1 [A]3 [C]1 [D]3 [E]5 [F]3 [H]1
[L]2 [M]1 [N]2 [O]1 [R]1 [S]3 [T]1 [U]1
[B]1 [C]1 [E]1 [H]1 [I]1 [O]2 [P]1 [R]2 [S]2 [T]2 [V]1 [—]1

**DON'T BE A
PEW POTATO.**
[']1 [.]1 [A]2 [B]1 [D]1
[E]2 [N]1 [O]3 [P]2 [T]3 [W]1

**CHRISTIANITY
MAY BE OLD,
BUT IT'S NEW
EVERY DAY.**
[']1 [,]1 [.]1 [A]3 [B]2 [C]1 [D]2 [E]4 [H]1 [I]4
[L]1 [M]1 [N]2 [O]1 [R]2 [S]2 [T]4 [U]1 [V]1 [W]1 [Y]4

EVERY NEW REVELATION
ABOUT GOD REQUIRES
A NEW DEDICATION
TO HIM.

[.]1 [A]4 [B]1 [C]1 [D]3 [E]9 [G]1 [H]1 [I]5 [L]1
[M]1 [N]4 [O]5 [Q]1 [R]4 [S]1 [T]4 [U]2 [V]2 [W]2 [Y]1

CONSTANT SUNSHINE
PRODUCES A DESERT.
— ANONYMOUS

[.]1 [A]2 [C]2 [D]2 [E]4 [H]1 [I]1
[N]4 [O]2 [P]1 [R]2 [S]5 [T]3 [U]2
[A]1 [M]1 [N]2 [O]2 [S]1 [U]1 [Y]1 [—]1

DISCIPLESHIP IS
LEARNING TO KEEP
OUR HAND IN HIS.
— ANONYMOUS

[.]1 [A]2 [C]1 [D]2 [E]4 [G]1 [H]3 [I]7
[K]1 [L]2 [N]4 [O]2 [P]3 [R]2 [S]4 [T]1 [U]1
[A]1 [M]1 [N]2 [O]2 [S]1 [U]1 [Y]1 [—]1

SAINTS UNDER
CONSTRUCTION

[A]1 [C]2 [D]1 [E]1 [I]2
[N]4 [O]2 [R]2 [S]3 [T]3 [U]2

THE ROAD TO
CHRIST'S KINGDOM
IS ALWAYS
UNDER CONSTRUCTION.

[']1 [.]1 [A]3 [C]3 [D]3 [E]2 [G]1 [H]2 [I]4 [K]1
[L]1 [M]1 [N]4 [O]5 [R]4 [S]5 [T]5 [U]2 [W]1 [Y]1

RIGHTEOUSNESS
IS A PATH,
NOT A PLACE.

[,]1 [.]1 [A]4 [C]1 [E]3 [G]1 [H]2 [I]2
[L]1 [N]2 [O]2 [P]2 [R]1 [S]4 [T]3 [U]1

CHANGE YOUR THOUGHTS
AND YOU CHANGE
YOUR WORLD.
— NORMAN VINCENT PEALE

[.]1 [A]3 [C]2 [D]2 [E]2 [G]3 [H]4 [L]1
[N]3 [O]5 [R]3 [S]1 [T]2 [U]4 [W]1 [Y]3
[A]2 [C]1 [E]3 [I]1 [L]1 [M]1 [N]4 [O]1 [P]1 [R]1 [T]1 [V]1 [—]1

EVERY TEST IS A CHANCE
TO LEAVE MORE OF OUR
OLD SELVES BEHIND.

[.]1 [A]3 [B]1 [C]2 [D]2 [E]10 [F]1 [H]2 [I]2
[L]3 [M]1 [N]2 [O]5 [R]3 [S]4 [T]3 [U]1 [V]3 [Y]1

WE'RE LED TO
BELIEVE IN HIM,
DRIVEN TO
BECOME LIKE HIM.

[']1 [,]1 [.]1 [B]2 [C]1 [D]2 [E]10 [H]2 [I]6
[K]1 [L]3 [M]3 [N]2 [O]3 [R]2 [T]2 [V]2 [W]1

Hard Work Works Wonders

Proverbs on persistence

WHEN WE REST,
WE RUST.
— GERMAN PROVERB
[,]1 [.]1 [E]4 [H]1 [N]1 [R]2 [S]2 [T]2 [U]1 [W]3
[A]1 [B]1 [E]2 [G]1 [M]1 [N]1 [O]1 [P]1 [R]3 [V]1 [—]1

HE WHO DOES NOTHING
BUT WAIT FOR HIS SHIP
TO COME IN HAS ALREADY
MISSED THE BOAT.
(*Wings of Silver*)
[.]1 [A]5 [B]2 [C]1 [D]3 [E]6 [F]1 [G]1 [H]7 [I]6
[L]1 [M]2 [N]3 [O]7 [P]1 [R]2 [S]6 [T]6 [U]1 [W]2 [Y]1

MAYBE YOU CAN'T
DO EVERYTHING, BUT
YOU CAN STILL
DO SOMETHING.
[']1 [,]1 [.]1 [A]3 [B]2 [C]2 [D]2 [E]4 [G]2 [H]2
[I]3 [L]2 [M]2 [N]4 [O]5 [R]1 [S]2 [T]5 [U]3 [V]1 [Y]4

GOD WILL SUPPLY,
BUT WE MUST APPLY.
(*Wings of Silver*)
[,]1 [.]1 [A]1 [B]1 [D]1 [E]1 [G]1 [I]1
[L]4 [M]1 [O]1 [P]4 [S]2 [T]2 [U]3 [W]2 [Y]2

IF YOU DON'T HAVE
TIME TO DO IT RIGHT,
YOU MUST HAVE TIME TO
DO IT OVER. — ANONYMOUS
[']1 [,]1 [.]1 [A]2 [D]3 [E]5 [F]1 [G]1 [H]3
[I]6 [M]3 [N]1 [O]8 [R]2 [S]1 [T]9 [U]3 [V]3 [Y]2
[A]1 [M]1 [N]2 [O]2 [S]1 [U]1 [Y]1 [—]1

DO WHAT YOU CAN,
WITH WHAT YOU HAVE,
WHERE YOU ARE.
— THEODORE ROOSEVELT
[,]2 [.]1 [A]5 [C]1 [D]1 [E]4 [H]5 [I]1
[N]1 [O]4 [R]2 [T]3 [U]3 [V]1 [W]4 [Y]3
[D]1 [E]4 [H]1 [L]1 [O]4 [R]2 [S]1 [T]2 [V]1 [—]1

DO NOT LET WHAT YOU
CANNOT DO INTERFERE
WITH WHAT YOU CAN DO.
— JOHN WOODEN
[.]1 [A]4 [C]2 [D]3 [E]4 [F]1 [H]3 [I]2
[L]1 [N]5 [O]7 [R]2 [T]7 [U]2 [W]3 [Y]2
[D]1 [E]1 [H]1 [J]1 [N]2 [O]3 [W]1 [—]1

S-L-O-T-H
SPELLS
TROUBLE.
[-]4 [.]1 [B]1 [E]2 [H]1 [L]4
[O]2 [P]1 [R]1 [S]3 [T]2 [U]1

**WE OFTEN MISS AN
OPPORTUNITY BECAUSE
IT LOOKS LIKE WORK.
— REVISED BEN FRANKLIN**

[.]1 [A]2 [B]1 [C]1 [E]5 [F]1 [I]4 [K]3 [L]2
[M]1 [N]3 [O]6 [P]2 [R]2 [S]4 [T]4 [U]2 [W]2 [Y]1
[A]1 [B]1 [D]1 [E]3 [F]1 [I]2 [K]1 [L]1 [N]3 [R]2 [S]1 [V]1 [—]1

**BE A CUT ABOVE —
OR PLAN TO
LOSE SOMETHING.**

[—]1 [.]1 [A]3 [B]2 [C]1 [E]4 [G]1 [H]1 [I]1
[L]2 [M]1 [N]2 [O]5 [P]1 [R]1 [S]2 [T]3 [U]1 [V]1

**IT'S NOT WHETHER YOU
GET KNOCKED DOWN. IT'S
WHETHER YOU GET
UP. — VINCE LOMBARDI**

[']2 [.]2 [C]1 [D]2 [E]7 [G]2 [H]4 [I]2 [K]2
[N]3 [O]5 [P]1 [R]2 [S]2 [T]7 [U]3 [W]3 [Y]2
[A]1 [B]1 [C]1 [D]1 [E]1 [I]2 [L]1 [M]1 [N]1 [O]1 [R]1 [V]1 [—]1

**TO MOVE THE WORLD,
YOU MUST FIRST
MOVE YOURSELF.
— SOCRATES**

[,]1 [.]1 [D]1 [E]4 [F]2 [H]1 [I]1 [L]2
[M]3 [O]6 [R]3 [S]3 [T]4 [U]3 [V]2 [W]1 [Y]2
[A]1 [C]1 [E]1 [O]1 [R]1 [S]2 [T]1 [—]1

**INCLUDE THE SUCCESS OF
OTHERS IN YOUR DREAMS
FOR YOUR OWN SUCCESS.
— ANONYMOUS**
[.]1 [A]1 [C]5 [D]2 [E]6 [F]2 [H]2 [I]2 [L]1
[M]1 [N]3 [O]6 [R]5 [S]8 [T]2 [U]5 [W]1 [Y]2
[A]1 [M]1 [N]2 [O]2 [S]1 [U]1 [Y]1 [—]1

**EXPERIENCE IS WHAT
YOU GET WHEN YOU WERE
EXPECTING SOMETHING
ELSE. — ANONYMOUS**
[.]1 [A]1 [C]2 [E]13 [G]3 [H]3 [I]4 [L]1 [M]1
[N]4 [O]3 [P]2 [R]2 [S]3 [T]4 [U]2 [W]3 [X]2 [Y]2
[A]1 [M]1 [N]2 [O]2 [S]1 [U]1 [Y]1 [—]1

**THE LORD WORKS
WONDERS WITH THOSE
WHO DON'T CARE WHO
GETS THE CREDIT.**
[']1 [.]1 [A]1 [C]2 [D]4 [E]7 [G]1 [H]6
[I]2 [K]1 [L]1 [N]2 [O]7 [R]5 [S]4 [T]7 [W]5

**FOOTPRINTS ON THE
SANDS OF TIME ARE
NEVER MADE BY SITTING
DOWN. — ANONYMOUS**
[.]1 [A]3 [B]1 [D]3 [E]6 [F]2 [G]1 [H]1 [I]4
[M]2 [N]6 [O]5 [P]1 [R]3 [S]4 [T]6 [V]1 [W]1 [Y]1
[A]1 [M]1 [N]2 [O]2 [S]1 [U]1 [Y]1 [—]1

**IF AT FIRST YOU
DO SUCCEED,
TRY SOMETHING HARDER.**
(*Wings of Silver*)
[,]1 [.]1 [A]2 [C]2 [D]3 [E]4 [F]2 [G]1 [H]2
[I]3 [M]1 [N]1 [O]3 [R]4 [S]3 [T]4 [U]2 [Y]2

**IN GREAT ATTEMPTS
IT IS GLORIOUS
EVEN TO FAIL.**
(*Wings of Silver*)
[.]1 [A]3 [E]4 [F]1 [G]2 [I]5 [L]2 [M]1
[N]2 [O]3 [P]1 [R]2 [S]3 [T]6 [U]1 [V]1

**FAILURE IS ONLY THE
CHANCE TO BEGIN AGAIN
MORE INTELLIGENTLY.**
— HENRY FORD
[.]1 [A]4 [B]1 [C]2 [E]7 [F]1 [G]3 [H]2 [I]6
[L]5 [M]1 [N]6 [O]3 [R]2 [S]1 [T]4 [U]1 [Y]2
[D]1 [E]1 [F]1 [H]1 [N]1 [O]1 [R]2 [Y]1 [—]1

**WHY NOT GO OUT ON A
LIMB? ISN'T THAT
WHERE THE FRUIT IS?**
— FRANK SCULLY
[']1 [?]2 [A]2 [B]1 [E]3 [F]1 [G]1 [H]4 [I]4
[L]1 [M]1 [N]3 [O]4 [R]2 [S]2 [T]7 [U]2 [W]2 [Y]1
[A]1 [C]1 [F]1 [K]1 [L]2 [N]1 [R]1 [S]1 [U]1 [Y]1 [—]1

TO BE A WINNER,
ALL IT TAKES IS
ALL YOU'VE GOT.
— ANONYMOUS

[']1 [,]1 [.]1 [A]4 [B]1 [E]4 [G]1 [I]3 [K]1
[L]4 [N]2 [O]3 [R]1 [S]2 [T]4 [U]1 [V]1 [W]1 [Y]1
[A]1 [M]1 [N]2 [O]2 [S]1 [U]1 [Y]1 [—]1

NEVER DESPAIR,
BUT IF YOU DO,
WORK ON IN DESPAIR.
(*Wings of Silver*)

[,]2 [.]1 [A]2 [B]1 [D]3 [E]4 [F]1 [I]4 [K]1
[N]3 [O]4 [P]2 [R]4 [S]2 [T]1 [U]2 [V]1 [W]1 [Y]1

FALL SEVEN TIMES,
STAND UP EIGHT.
— JAPANESE PROVERB

[,]1 [.]1 [A]2 [D]1 [E]4 [F]1 [G]1 [H]1
[I]2 [L]2 [M]1 [N]2 [P]1 [S]3 [T]3 [U]1 [V]1
[A]2 [B]1 [E]3 [J]1 [N]1 [O]1 [P]2 [R]2 [S]1 [V]1 [—]1

WHETHER YOU THINK
YOU CAN OR THINK
YOU CAN'T, YOU'RE
RIGHT. — HENRY FORD

[']2 [,]1 [.]1 [A]2 [C]2 [E]3 [G]1 [H]5
[I]3 [K]2 [N]4 [O]5 [R]4 [T]5 [U]4 [W]1 [Y]4
[D]1 [E]1 [F]1 [H]1 [N]1 [O]1 [R]2 [Y]1 [—]1

IF YOU WANT
YOUR DREAMS TO
COME TRUE,
DON'T SLEEP.
(*Wings of Silver*)
   [']1 [,]1 [.]1 [A]2 [C]1 [D]2 [E]5 [F]1 [I]1 [L]1
   [M]2 [N]2 [O]5 [P]1 [R]3 [S]2 [T]4 [U]3 [W]1 [Y]2

Highest Hopes

Aphorisms on optimism

HOPE: THE FEELING
YOU HAVE THAT
THE FEELING YOU HAVE
ISN'T PERMANENT.
— ANONYMOUS
   [']1 [.]1 [:]1 [A]4 [E]11 [F]2 [G]2 [H]6 [I]3 [L]2
   [M]1 [N]5 [O]3 [P]2 [R]1 [S]1 [T]6 [U]2 [V]2 [Y]2
   [A]1 [M]1 [N]2 [O]2 [S]1 [U]1 [Y]1 [—]1

WHEN LIFE LOOMS LARGE,
REMEMBER THAT GOD'S
LARGER THAN LIFE.
   [']1 [,]1 [.]1 [A]4 [B]1 [D]1 [E]8 [F]2 [G]3
   [H]3 [I]2 [L]5 [M]3 [N]2 [O]3 [R]5 [S]2 [T]3 [W]1

DON'T GO TO THE
WISHING WELL, BUT
THE LIVING WELL.
   [']1 [,]1 [.]1 [B]1 [D]1 [E]4 [G]3 [H]3
   [I]4 [L]5 [N]3 [O]3 [S]1 [T]5 [U]1 [V]1 [W]3

YOU'VE GOT FRIENDS
IN HIGH PLACES.
   [']1 [.]1 [A]1 [C]1 [D]1 [E]3 [F]1 [G]2 [H]2 [I]3
   [L]1 [N]2 [O]2 [P]1 [R]1 [S]2 [T]1 [U]1 [V]1 [Y]1

NOT TO OURS,
BUT TO THE BEST
OF HIS ABILITY.

[,]1 [.]1 [A]1 [B]3 [E]2 [F]1 [H]2 [I]3
[L]1 [N]1 [O]5 [R]1 [S]3 [T]7 [U]2 [Y]1

ONE DAY WE'LL ALL
BE HOME FREE.

[']1 [.]1 [A]2 [B]1 [D]1 [E]6 [F]1
[H]1 [L]4 [M]1 [N]1 [O]2 [R]1 [W]1 [Y]1

WHEN YOU'RE DOWN
AND OUT, SOMETHING
ALWAYS TURNS UP.
— ORSON WELLES

[']1 [,]1 [.]1 [A]3 [D]2 [E]3 [G]1 [H]2 [I]1 [L]1
[M]1 [N]5 [O]4 [P]1 [R]2 [S]3 [T]3 [U]4 [W]3 [Y]2
[E]2 [L]2 [N]1 [O]2 [R]1 [S]2 [W]1 [—]1

CHRIST, THE
HOPE OF GLORY.
— COLOSSIANS 1:27

[,]1 [—]1 [.]1 [1]1 [2]1 [7]1 [:]1 [A]1 [C]2 [E]2 [F]1
[G]1 [H]3 [I]2 [L]2 [N]1 [O]5 [P]1 [R]2 [S]4 [T]2 [Y]1

AS FAR AS THE
MASTER'S CONCERNED,
YOU'RE A MASTERPIECE
IN THE MAKING.

[']2 [,]1 [.]1 [A]7 [C]3 [D]1 [E]9 [F]1 [G]1 [H]2
[I]3 [K]1 [M]3 [N]4 [O]2 [P]1 [R]5 [S]5 [T]4 [U]1 [Y]1

**HOPE THAT IS SEEN
IS NO HOPE AT ALL.
— ROMANS 8:24**
    [—]1 [.]1 [2]1 [4]1 [8]1 [:]1 [A]4 [E]4 [H]3
    [I]2 [L]2 [M]1 [N]3 [O]4 [P]2 [R]1 [S]4 [T]3

**HOPE, THE PATENT
MEDICINE FOR DISEASE,
DISASTER, SIN.
— WALLACE RICE**
    [,]3 [.]1 [A]3 [C]1 [D]3 [E]8 [F]1 [H]2
    [I]5 [M]1 [N]3 [O]2 [P]2 [R]2 [S]5 [T]4
    [A]2 [C]2 [E]2 [I]1 [L]2 [R]1 [W]1 [—]1

**BECAUSE OUR HOPE IS
IN HIM, THE WORLD'S
HOPE IS IN US.**
    [']1 [,]1 [.]1 [A]1 [B]1 [C]1 [D]1 [E]5 [H]4 [I]5
    [L]1 [M]1 [N]2 [O]4 [P]2 [R]2 [S]5 [T]1 [U]3 [W]1

**IF YOU'VE RUN INTO
A PASSLE OF HASSLES,
ROPE A HOPE.**
    [']1 [,]1 [.]1 [A]4 [E]5 [F]2 [H]2 [I]2 [L]2
    [N]2 [O]5 [P]3 [R]2 [S]5 [T]1 [U]2 [V]1 [Y]1

**FAITH IS THE
SUBSTANCE OF
THINGS HOPED FOR.
— HEBREWS 11:1**
    [—]1 [.]1 [1]3 [:]1 [A]2 [B]2 [C]1 [D]1 [E]5 [F]3
    [G]1 [H]5 [I]3 [N]2 [O]3 [P]1 [R]2 [S]5 [T]4 [U]1 [W]1

Human Nature

Homo sapiens: The horror and the humor

**DON'T BE
A HURRYWART.**
   [']1 [.]1 [A]2 [B]1 [D]1 [E]1 [H]1
   [N]1 [O]1 [R]3 [T]2 [U]1 [W]1 [Y]1

**WE'RE ALL FAILERS;
WE'RE NONE OF
US FAILURES.
— LARRY ALLGOOD**
   [']2 [.]1 [;]1 [A]3 [E]7 [F]3 [I]2
   [L]4 [N]2 [O]2 [R]4 [S]3 [U]2 [W]2
   [A]2 [D]1 [G]1 [L]3 [O]2 [R]2 [Y]1 [—]1

**THE MORE YOU SEE
A TEMPTATION,
THE BETTER IT LOOKS.
— ANONYMOUS**
   [,]1 [.]1 [A]2 [B]1 [E]8 [H]2 [I]2 [K]1 [L]1
   [M]2 [N]1 [O]5 [P]1 [R]2 [S]2 [T]8 [U]1 [Y]1
   [A]1 [M]1 [N]2 [O]2 [S]1 [U]1 [Y]1 [—]1

**JESUS TURNED WATER
INTO WINE, BUT HE CAN'T
TURN WHINING INTO
ANYTHING. — MARK STEELE**
   [']1 [,]1 [.]1 [A]3 [B]1 [C]1 [D]1 [E]5 [G]2 [H]3
   [I]6 [J]1 [N]10 [O]2 [R]3 [S]2 [T]8 [U]4 [W]3 [Y]1
   [A]1 [E]3 [K]1 [L]1 [M]1 [R]1 [S]1 [T]1 [—]1

THOSE WHO COVET
MEGABUCKS SHOULD
UPGRADE THEIR
INTERNAL DRIVES.

[.]1 [A]3 [B]1 [C]2 [D]3 [E]7 [G]2 [H]4 [I]3 [K]1
[L]2 [M]1 [N]2 [O]4 [P]1 [R]4 [S]4 [T]4 [U]3 [V]2 [W]1

THE WAGES OF SIN
IS DEATH; 'TIL THEN,
IT'S LIFE IN PRISON.

[']2 [,]1 [.]1 [;]1 [A]2 [D]1 [E]5 [F]2 [G]1
[H]3 [I]7 [L]2 [N]4 [O]2 [P]1 [R]1 [S]5 [T]5 [W]1

NINETY PERCENT OF THE
FRICTION OF DAILY LIFE
IS CAUSED BY THE
WRONG TONE OF VOICE.
(*Wings of Silver*)

[.]1 [A]2 [B]1 [C]4 [D]2 [E]9 [F]5 [G]1 [H]2 [I]7
[L]2 [N]6 [O]7 [P]1 [R]3 [S]2 [T]6 [U]1 [V]1 [W]1 [Y]3

WHY ARE GOOD HABITS
SO MUCH EASIER
TO GIVE UP
THAN BAD ONES?

[?]1 [A]5 [B]2 [C]1 [D]2 [E]5 [G]2 [H]4 [I]3 [M]1
[N]2 [O]5 [P]1 [R]2 [S]4 [T]3 [U]2 [V]1 [W]1 [Y]1

THERE IS NOT A JUST
MAN ON EARTH WHO DOES
GOOD AND SINS NOT.
— ECCLESIASTES 7:20
[—]1 [.]1 [0]1 [2]1 [7]1 [:]1 [A]5 [C]2 [D]3 [E]7 [G]1
[H]3 [I]3 [J]1 [L]1 [M]1 [N]6 [O]7 [R]2 [S]8 [T]6 [U]1 [W]1

TO THE HUNGRY SOUL,
EVERY BITTER THING
IS SWEET.
— PROVERBS 27:7
[,]1 [—]1 [.]1 [2]1 [7]2 [:]1 [B]2 [E]7 [G]2 [H]3 [I]3
[L]1 [N]2 [O]3 [P]1 [R]5 [S]4 [T]6 [U]2 [V]2 [W]1 [Y]2

THOSE WHO PLANT
GREED WILL REAP
A "MINE" FIELD.
["]1 ["]1 [.]1 [A]3 [D]2 [E]6 [F]1 [G]1 [H]2 [I]3
[L]4 [M]1 [N]2 [O]2 [P]2 [R]2 [S]1 [T]2 [W]2

WOULD WE RATHER BE
RUINED BY PRAISE OR
SAVED BY CRITICISM?
[?]1 [A]3 [B]3 [C]2 [D]3 [E]6 [H]1 [I]5 [L]1 [M]1
[N]1 [O]2 [P]1 [R]6 [S]3 [T]2 [U]2 [V]2 [W]1 [Y]2

BETTER TO BITE YOUR
TONGUE NOW THAN HAVE TO
EAT YOUR WORDS LATER.
[.]1 [A]4 [B]2 [D]1 [E]7 [G]1 [H]2 [I]1 [L]1
[N]3 [O]7 [R]5 [S]1 [T]9 [U]3 [V]1 [W]2 [Y]2

WHAT WE NEED
ISN'T MORE GOOD
PREACHING BUT MORE
GOOD HEARING.
['] 1 [.]1 [A]3 [B]1 [C]1 [D]3 [E]7 [G]4 [H]3
[I]3 [M]2 [N]4 [O]6 [P]1 [R]4 [S]1 [T]3 [U]1 [W]2

IT IS GREAT TO BE
GREAT, BUT IT IS
GREATER TO BE HUMAN.
— WILL ROGERS
[,]1 [.]1 [A]4 [B]3 [E]6 [G]3 [H]1
[I]4 [M]1 [N]1 [O]2 [R]4 [S]2 [T]8 [U]2
[E]1 [G]1 [I]1 [L]2 [O]1 [R]2 [S]1 [W]1 [—]1

GOSSIP LEAVES
A BAD TASTE IN
EVERYONE'S MOUTH.
['] 1 [.]1 [A]4 [B]1 [D]1 [E]6 [G]1 [H]1 [I]2 [L]1
[M]1 [N]2 [O]3 [P]1 [R]1 [S]5 [T]3 [U]1 [V]2 [Y]1

IT'S EASIER TO REPENT
OF SINS WE'VE COMMITTED
THAN THOSE WE INTEND
TO. — JOSH BILLINGS
['] 2 [.]1 [A]2 [C]1 [D]2 [E]10 [F]1 [H]2 [I]5
[M]2 [N]5 [O]5 [P]1 [R]2 [S]5 [T]9 [V]1 [W]2
[B]1 [G]1 [H]1 [I]2 [J]1 [L]2 [N]1 [O]1 [S]2 [—]1

IF YOU PUT A SMALL
VALUE ON YOURSELF, THE
WORLD WILL NOT RAISE
YOUR PRICE. — ANONYMOUS

[,]1 [.]1 [A]4 [C]1 [D]1 [E]5 [F]2 [H]1 [I]4 [L]7
[M]1 [N]2 [O]6 [P]2 [R]5 [S]3 [T]3 [U]5 [V]1 [W]2 [Y]3
[A]1 [M]1 [N]2 [O]2 [S]1 [U]1 [Y]1 [—]1

TOO MANY PEOPLE ARE
READY TO CARRY THE STOOL
WHEN THE PIANO NEEDS
TO BE MOVED. — ANONYMOUS

[.]1 [A]5 [B]1 [C]1 [D]3 [E]11 [H]3 [I]1 [L]2
[M]2 [N]4 [O]9 [P]3 [R]4 [S]2 [T]6 [V]1 [W]1 [Y]3
[A]1 [M]1 [N]2 [O]2 [S]1 [U]1 [Y]1 [—]1

IF ALL YOU HAVE
IS A HAMMER,
EVERYTHING LOOKS
LIKE A NAIL. — ANONYMOUS

[,]1 [.]1 [A]6 [E]5 [F]1 [G]1 [H]3 [I]5 [K]2
[L]5 [M]2 [N]2 [O]3 [R]2 [S]2 [T]1 [U]1 [V]2 [Y]2
[A]1 [M]1 [N]2 [O]2 [S]1 [U]1 [Y]1 [—]1

A GOOD SERMON LEAVES
YOU WONDERING HOW THE
PREACHER KNEW ALL
ABOUT YOU. — ANONYMOUS

[.]1 [A]5 [B]1 [C]1 [D]2 [E]8 [G]2 [H]3 [I]1 [K]1 [L]3
[M]1 [N]4 [O]8 [P]1 [R]4 [S]2 [T]2 [U]3 [V]1 [W]3 [Y]2
[A]1 [M]1 [N]2 [O]2 [S]1 [U]1 [Y]1 [—]1

EVERY TIME HISTORY
REPEATS ITSELF,
THE PRICE GOES UP.
— ANONYMOUS
  [,]1 [.]1 [A]1 [C]1 [E]9 [F]1 [G]1 [H]2 [I]4
  [L]1 [M]1 [O]2 [P]3 [R]4 [S]4 [T]5 [U]1 [V]1 [Y]2
  [A]1 [M]1 [N]2 [O]2 [S]1 [U]1 [Y]1 [—]1

THE DIFFERENCE BETWEEN
GENIUS AND IGNORANCE
IS THAT GENIUS HAS
ITS LIMITS. — ANONYMOUS
  [.]1 [A]4 [B]1 [C]2 [D]2 [E]10 [F]2 [G]3 [H]3
  [I]8 [L]1 [M]1 [N]7 [O]1 [R]2 [S]6 [T]6 [U]2 [W]1
  [A]1 [M]1 [N]2 [O]2 [S]1 [U]1 [Y]1 [—]1

CONSCIENCE IS WHAT
HURTS WHEN EVERYTHING
ELSE FEELS SO GOOD.
— ANONYMOUS
  [.]1 [A]1 [C]3 [D]1 [E]9 [F]1 [G]2 [H]4 [I]3
  [L]2 [N]4 [O]4 [R]2 [S]6 [T]3 [U]1 [V]1 [W]2 [Y]1
  [A]1 [M]1 [N]2 [O]2 [S]1 [U]1 [Y]1 [—]1

EVE TAUGHT US
IT'S OKAY TO TAKE
A LITTLE RIBBING.
  [']1 [.]1 [A]4 [B]2 [E]4 [G]2 [H]1 [I]4 [K]2
  [L]2 [N]1 [O]2 [R]1 [S]2 [T]7 [U]2 [V]1 [Y]1

**TO BELITTLE
IS TO BE LITTLE.**
(*Wings of Silver*)
    [.]1 [B]2 [E]4 [I]3 [L]4 [O]2 [S]1 [T]6

**RELIGION MAY NOT KEEP
YOU FROM SINNING,
BUT IT TAKES
THE JOY OUT OF IT.**
(*Wings of Silver*)
    [,]1 [.]1 [A]2 [B]1 [E]5 [F]2 [G]2 [H]1 [I]6 [J]1
    [K]2 [L]1 [M]2 [N]5 [O]7 [P]1 [R]2 [S]2 [T]7 [U]3 [Y]3

**ALMOST ANYTHING
IS EASIER TO GET
INTO THAN OUT OF.
— ALLEN'S LAW**
    [.]1 [A]4 [E]3 [F]1 [G]2 [H]2 [I]4 [L]1
    [M]1 [N]4 [O]5 [R]1 [S]3 [T]7 [U]1 [Y]1
    [']1 [A]2 [E]1 [L]3 [N]1 [S]1 [W]1 [—]1

**LIFE IS A
METTLE
DETECTOR.**
    [.]1 [A]1 [C]1 [D]1 [E]5 [F]1
    [I]2 [L]2 [M]1 [O]1 [R]1 [S]1 [T]4

**ADVICE WOULD BE MORE
ACCEPTABLE IF IT DIDN'T
ALWAYS CONFLICT WITH
OUR PLANS. — ANONYMOUS**
[']1 [.]1 [A]6 [B]2 [C]5 [D]4 [E]5 [F]2 [H]1 [I]6 [L]5
[M]1 [N]3 [O]4 [P]2 [R]2 [S]2 [T]5 [U]2 [V]1 [W]3 [Y]1
[A]1 [M]1 [N]2 [O]2 [S]1 [U]1 [Y]1 [—]1

**WE HAVE THE WILL
TO RESIST BOTH
GOOD AND EVIL.**
[.]1 [A]2 [B]1 [D]2 [E]5 [G]1 [H]3 [I]3
[L]3 [N]1 [O]4 [R]1 [S]2 [T]4 [V]2 [W]2

**THERE'S A REASON
IT'S CALLED
FOOLING AROUND.**
[']2 [.]1 [A]4 [C]1 [D]2 [E]4 [F]1 [G]1
[H]1 [I]2 [L]3 [N]3 [O]4 [R]3 [S]3 [T]2 [U]1

**GAMBLING LEAVES
ONE A LITTLE BLUE
AROUND THE BILLS.**
[.]1 [A]4 [B]3 [D]1 [E]6 [G]2 [H]1 [I]3
[L]7 [M]1 [N]3 [O]2 [R]1 [S]2 [T]3 [U]2 [V]1

**SOMETIMES OUR
PRIDE KEEPS
GOD'S LOVE AT
ARM'S LENGTH.**
[']2 [.]1 [A]2 [D]2 [E]7 [G]2 [H]1 [I]2 [K]1
[L]2 [M]3 [N]1 [O]4 [P]2 [R]3 [S]5 [T]3 [U]1 [V]1

WE SHOULD PUT OUR
SIN AT HIS DISPOSAL.

[.]1 [A]2 [D]2 [E]1 [H]2 [I]3 [L]2
[N]1 [O]3 [P]2 [R]1 [S]5 [T]2 [U]3 [W]1

SOME ARE WISE AND
SOME ARE OTHERWISE.
— ANONYMOUS

[.]1 [A]3 [D]1 [E]7 [H]1 [I]2
[M]2 [N]1 [O]3 [R]3 [S]4 [T]1 [W]2
[A]1 [M]1 [N]2 [O]2 [S]1 [U]1 [Y]1 [—]1

IF SERVING OTHERS IS
BENEATH YOU, YOU'RE
NOT ON TOP OF THINGS.

[']1 [,]1 [.]1 [A]1 [B]1 [E]5 [F]2 [G]2 [H]3
[I]4 [N]5 [O]7 [P]1 [R]3 [S]4 [T]5 [U]2 [V]1 [Y]2

TURN A COLD SHOULDER
TO HOT GOSSIP.

[.]1 [A]1 [C]1 [D]2 [E]1 [G]1 [H]2 [I]1
[L]2 [N]1 [O]5 [P]1 [R]2 [S]3 [T]3 [U]2

ABSTINENCE MAKES THE
HEART GROW FONDER.

[.]1 [A]3 [B]1 [C]1 [D]1 [E]6 [F]1 [G]1 [H]2
[I]1 [K]1 [M]1 [N]3 [O]2 [R]3 [S]2 [T]3 [W]1

NEVER RUN FASTER
THAN YOUR GUARDIAN
ANGEL CAN FLY.
— ANONYMOUS

[.]1 [A]6 [C]1 [D]1 [E]4 [F]2 [G]2 [H]1 [I]1
[L]2 [N]6 [O]1 [R]5 [S]1 [T]2 [U]3 [V]1 [Y]2
[A]1 [M]1 [N]2 [O]2 [S]1 [U]1 [Y]1 [—]1

IT'S HARD TO FIND
THE ANSWERS WHEN
WE THINK WE ALREADY
HAVE THEM ALL.

[']1 [.]1 [A]6 [D]3 [E]8 [F]1 [H]6 [I]3 [K]1
[L]3 [M]1 [N]4 [O]1 [R]3 [S]3 [T]5 [V]1 [W]4 [Y]1

RESTLESSNESS IS
DISSATISFACTION
GUARANTEED.

[.]1 [A]4 [C]1 [D]2 [E]5 [F]1 [G]1
[I]4 [L]1 [N]3 [O]1 [R]2 [S]9 [T]4 [U]1

TALK ENOUGH TRASH
AND YOU'LL SOON BE
IN THE DUMPS.

[']1 [.]1 [A]3 [B]1 [D]2 [E]3 [G]1 [H]3 [I]1 [K]1
[L]3 [M]1 [N]4 [O]4 [P]1 [R]1 [S]3 [T]3 [U]3 [Y]1

**HE WHO IS ALL
WRAPPED UP IN HIMSELF
IS OVERDRESSED.
— ANONYMOUS**
> [.]1 [A]2 [D]3 [E]6 [F]1 [H]3 [I]4 [L]3
> [M]1 [N]1 [O]2 [P]3 [R]3 [S]5 [U]1 [V]1 [W]2
> [A]1 [M]1 [N]2 [O]2 [S]1 [U]1 [Y]1 [—]1

**WITHOUT FAIL,
WE DO,
BUT HE DOESN'T.**
> [']1 [,]2 [.]1 [A]1 [B]1 [D]2 [E]3 [F]1
> [H]2 [I]2 [L]1 [N]1 [O]3 [S]1 [T]4 [U]2 [W]2

**IF PRIDE GOES BEFORE
A FALL, HUMILITY
SHOULD ARRIVE
BY THAT WINTER.**
> [,]1 [.]1 [A]4 [B]2 [D]2 [E]6 [F]3 [G]1 [H]3 [I]6 [L]4
> [M]1 [N]1 [O]3 [P]1 [R]5 [S]2 [T]4 [U]2 [V]1 [W]1 [Y]2

**OUR WILL IS FREE.
IT'S OUR DECISIONS
WE PAY FOR.**
> [']1 [.]2 [A]1 [C]1 [D]1 [E]4 [F]2 [I]5 [L]2
> [N]1 [O]4 [P]1 [R]4 [S]4 [T]1 [U]2 [W]2 [Y]1

**A LITTLE RELIGION
IS A DANGEROUS THING.**
> [.]1 [A]3 [D]1 [E]3 [G]3 [H]1 [I]5
> [L]3 [N]3 [O]2 [R]2 [S]2 [T]3 [U]1

In A Family Way

Home-grown truisms for today's nuclear unit

LET THEM LEARN FIRST
TO SHOW PIETY
AT HOME.
— 1 TIMOTHY 5:4
[—]1 [.]1 [1]1 [4]1 [5]1 [:]1 [A]2 [E]5 [F]1 [H]4
[I]3 [L]2 [M]3 [N]1 [O]4 [P]1 [R]2 [S]2 [T]8 [W]1 [Y]2

IF YOU DON'T HAVE TIME
FOR YOUR FAMILY, ARE
YOU SURE YOU'RE
FOLLOWING GOD'S WILL?
[']3 [,]1 [?]1 [A]3 [D]2 [E]5 [F]4 [G]2 [H]1 [I]5
[L]5 [M]2 [N]2 [O]9 [R]5 [S]2 [T]2 [U]5 [V]1 [W]2 [Y]5

HE THAT TROUBLETH
HIS OWN HOUSE
SHALL INHERIT THE WIND.
— PROVERBS 11:29
[—]1 [.]1 [1]2 [2]1 [9]1 [:]1 [A]2 [B]2 [D]1 [E]6 [H]8
[I]4 [L]3 [N]3 [O]4 [P]1 [R]4 [S]4 [T]6 [U]2 [V]1 [W]2

KINDNESS GOES A LONG
WAY LOTS OF TIMES
WHEN IT OUGHT TO STAY
AT HOME. — KIN HUBBARD
[.]1 [A]4 [D]1 [E]5 [F]1 [G]3 [H]3 [I]3 [K]1
[L]2 [M]2 [N]4 [O]7 [S]6 [T]7 [U]1 [W]2 [Y]2
[A]1 [B]2 [D]1 [H]1 [I]1 [K]1 [N]1 [R]1 [U]1 [—]1

HOME WASN'T
BUILT IN A DAY.
[']1 [.]1 [A]3 [B]1 [D]1 [E]1 [H]1 [I]2
[L]1 [M]1 [N]2 [O]1 [S]1 [T]2 [U]1 [W]1 [Y]1

DADS, DON'T EXASPERATE
YOUR KIDS, OR THEY'LL
GET DISCOURAGED.
— COLOSSIANS 3:21
[']2 [,]2 [—]1 [.]1 [1]1 [2]1 [3]1 [:]1 [A]5 [C]2 [D]6 [E]6 [G]2
[H]1 [I]3 [K]1 [L]3 [N]2 [O]6 [P]1 [R]4 [S]7 [T]4 [U]2 [X]1 [Y]2

YOUR CHILDREN NEED
YOUR PRESENCE MORE
THAN YOUR PRESENTS.
— JESSE JACKSON
[.]1 [A]1 [C]2 [D]2 [E]9 [H]2 [I]1 [L]1
[M]1 [N]5 [O]4 [P]2 [R]7 [S]3 [T]2 [U]3 [Y]3
[A]1 [C]1 [E]2 [J]2 [K]1 [N]1 [O]1 [S]3 [—]1

IT TAKES TWO TO MAKE
A MARRIAGE A SUCCESS
BUT ONLY ONE TO MAKE
IT A FAILURE. — H. SAMUEL
[.]1 [A]9 [B]1 [C]2 [E]7 [F]1 [G]1 [I]4 [K]3
[L]2 [M]3 [N]2 [O]5 [R]3 [S]4 [T]7 [U]3 [W]1 [Y]1
[.]1 [A]1 [E]1 [H]1 [L]1 [M]1 [S]1 [U]1 [—]1

SPOIL YOUR SPOUSE,
NOT YOUR CHILDREN.
— H. JACKSON BROWN, JR.

[,]1 [.]1 [C]1 [D]1 [E]2 [H]1 [I]2 [L]2
[N]2 [O]5 [P]2 [R]3 [S]3 [T]1 [U]3 [Y]2
[,]1 [.]2 [A]1 [B]1 [C]1 [H]1 [J]2 [K]1 [N]2 [O]2 [R]2 [S]1 [W]1 [—]1

TOO MANY
SPOUSES TAKE A
WAIT-AND-SEE THE
ATTITUDE.

[-]2 [.]1 [A]6 [D]2 [E]6 [H]1 [I]2 [K]1
[M]1 [N]2 [O]3 [P]1 [S]4 [T]7 [U]2 [W]1 [Y]1

CHILDREN
SPELL LOVE T-I-M-E.
— ANONYMOUS

[-]3 [.]1 [C]1 [D]1 [E]4 [H]1 [I]2 [L]4
[M]1 [N]1 [O]1 [P]1 [R]1 [S]1 [T]1 [V]1
[A]1 [M]1 [N]2 [O]2 [S]1 [U]1 [Y]1 [—]1

IT TAKES FIVE GOOD
EXCHANGES WITH YOUR
SPOUSE TO OFFSET
EACH BAD ONE.

[.]1 [A]4 [B]1 [C]2 [D]2 [E]8 [F]3 [G]2 [H]3 [I]3 [K]1
[N]2 [O]7 [P]1 [R]1 [S]5 [T]5 [U]2 [V]1 [W]1 [X]1 [Y]1

WHOEVER THINKS
MARRIAGE IS 50-50,
DOESN'T KNOW THE HALF
OF IT. (IT'S 100-100.)

[']2 [(]1 [)]1 [,]1 [-]2 [.]2 [0]6 [1]2 [5]2 [A]3 [D]1 [E]5 [F]2
[G]1 [H]4 [I]5 [K]2 [L]1 [M]1 [N]3 [O]4 [R]3 [S]4 [T]5 [V]1 [W]2

It Takes All Kindnesses

The nice thing about being a Christian

**KINDNESS IS IN OUR
POWER, EVEN WHEN
FONDNESS IS NOT.**
— SAMUEL JOHNSON
[,]1 [.]1 [D]2 [E]6 [F]1 [H]1 [I]4 [K]1
[N]8 [O]4 [P]1 [R]2 [S]6 [T]1 [U]1 [V]1 [W]2
[A]1 [E]1 [H]1 [J]1 [L]1 [M]1 [N]2 [O]2 [S]2 [U]1 [—]1

**NO MAN IS SO POOR
AS TO HAVE NOTHING
WORTH GIVING.**
— LONGFELLOW
[.]1 [A]3 [E]1 [G]3 [H]3 [I]4 [M]1
[N]5 [O]7 [P]1 [R]2 [S]3 [T]3 [V]2 [W]1
[E]1 [F]1 [G]1 [L]3 [N]1 [O]2 [W]1 [—]1

**WE MAKE A LIVING BY
WHAT WE GET. WE MAKE
A LIFE BY WHAT WE GIVE.**
— CHURCHILL
[.]2 [A]6 [B]2 [E]9 [F]1 [G]3 [H]2 [I]4
[K]2 [L]2 [M]2 [N]1 [T]3 [V]2 [W]6 [Y]2
[C]2 [H]2 [I]1 [L]2 [R]1 [U]1 [—]1

**MAKE FRIENDS
AS EASY AS "HI!"**
[!]1 ["]1 ["]1 [A]4 [D]1 [E]3 [F]1 [H]1
[I]2 [K]1 [M]1 [N]1 [R]1 [S]4 [Y]1

GO ON A FRIEND BINGE.

[.]1 [A]1 [B]1 [D]1 [E]2
[F]1 [G]2 [I]2 [N]3 [O]2 [R]1

NO ONE EVER DIED
FROM TOO MUCH PRAISE.
(*Wings of Silver*)

[.]1 [A]1 [C]1 [D]2 [E]5 [F]1 [H]1 [I]2
[M]2 [N]2 [O]5 [P]1 [R]3 [S]1 [T]1 [U]1 [V]1

ONE KIND WORD
CAN WARM THREE
WINTER MONTHS.
— JAPANESE PROVERB

[.]1 [A]2 [C]1 [D]2 [E]4 [H]2 [I]2
[K]1 [M]2 [N]5 [O]3 [R]4 [S]1 [T]3 [W]3
[A]2 [B]1 [E]3 [J]1 [N]1 [O]1 [P]2 [R]2 [S]1 [V]1 [—]1

ONE DOES EVIL
ENOUGH WHEN ONE
DOES NOTHING GOOD.
— GERMAN PROVERB

[.]1 [D]3 [E]7 [G]3 [H]3 [I]2 [L]1
[N]6 [O]8 [S]2 [T]1 [U]1 [V]1 [W]1
[A]1 [B]1 [E]2 [G]1 [M]1 [N]1 [O]1 [P]1 [R]3 [V]1 [—]1

BE KIND
TO UNKIND PEOPLE.
THEY NEED IT THE MOST.
— ANONYMOUS

[.]2 [B]1 [D]3 [E]7 [H]2 [I]3 [K]2 [L]1
[M]1 [N]4 [O]3 [P]2 [S]1 [T]5 [U]1 [Y]1
[A]1 [M]1 [N]2 [O]2 [S]1 [U]1 [Y]1 [—]1

MANNERS ARE
MINOR MORALS.
(*Wings of Silver*)
[.]1 [A]3 [E]2 [I]1 [L]1
[M]3 [N]3 [O]2 [R]4 [S]2

A SMALL UNKINDNESS
IS A GREAT OFFENSE.
(*Wings of Silver*)
[.]1 [A]4 [D]1 [E]4 [F]2 [G]1 [I]2 [K]1
[L]2 [M]1 [N]4 [O]1 [R]1 [S]5 [T]1 [U]1

TREES DON'T PRODUCE
FRUIT FOR THEMSELVES.
[']1 [.]1 [C]1 [D]2 [E]6 [F]2 [H]1 [I]1 [L]1
[M]1 [N]1 [O]3 [P]1 [R]4 [S]3 [T]4 [U]2 [V]1

WE ENTERTAIN
ANGELS UNAWARE.
SO BE NICE.
[.]2 [A]4 [B]1 [C]1 [E]7 [G]1 [I]2
[L]1 [N]5 [O]1 [R]2 [S]2 [T]2 [U]1 [W]2

NEVER LOOK DOWN
ON SOMEONE UNLESS
YOU'RE HELPING HIM UP.
— JESSE JACKSON
[']1 [.]1 [D]1 [E]7 [G]1 [H]2 [I]2 [K]1 [L]3
[M]2 [N]6 [O]7 [P]2 [R]2 [S]3 [U]3 [V]1 [W]1 [Y]1
[A]1 [C]1 [E]2 [J]2 [K]1 [N]1 [O]1 [S]3 [—]1

**GOT THE MILK OF
HUMAN KINDNESS?**
[?]1 [A]1 [D]1 [E]2 [F]1 [G]1 [H]2 [I]2
[K]2 [L]1 [M]2 [N]3 [O]2 [S]2 [T]2 [U]1

**RENDER YOUR OWN
TENDER MERCIES.**
[.]1 [C]1 [D]2 [E]6 [I]1 [M]1 [N]3
[O]2 [R]5 [S]1 [T]1 [U]1 [W]1 [Y]1

**KINDNESS IS
CHRISTIANITY WITH
ITS WORKING CLOTHES
ON. — ANONYMOUS**
[.]1 [A]1 [C]2 [D]1 [E]2 [G]1 [H]3 [I]8
[K]2 [L]1 [N]5 [O]3 [R]2 [S]6 [T]5 [W]2 [Y]1
[A]1 [M]1 [N]2 [O]2 [S]1 [U]1 [Y]1 [—]1

**IT IS KINDNESS IN
A PERSON, NOT BEAUTY,
WHICH WINS OUR
LOVE. — ANONYMOUS**
[,]2 [.]1 [A]2 [B]1 [C]1 [D]1 [E]4 [H]2 [I]6 [K]1
[L]1 [N]6 [O]4 [P]1 [R]2 [S]5 [T]3 [U]2 [V]1 [W]2 [Y]1
[A]1 [M]1 [N]2 [O]2 [S]1 [U]1 [Y]1 [—]1

Not To Worry

Axioms for the anxious

**WORRY'S
A REAL
TRUST-BUSTER.**
['] 1 [-]1 [.]1 [A]2 [B]1 [E]2 [L]1
[O]1 [R]5 [S]3 [T]3 [U]2 [W]1 [Y]1

**TWO DAYS TO KEEP
WORRY-FREE: TODAY
AND TOMORROW. — REVISED
ROBERT JONES BURDETT**
[-]1 [.]1 [:]1 [A]3 [D]3 [E]4 [F]1 [K]1
[M]1 [N]1 [O]7 [P]1 [R]5 [S]1 [T]4 [W]3 [Y]3
[B]2 [D]2 [E]5 [I]1 [J]1 [N]1 [O]2 [R]4 [S]2 [T]3 [U]1 [V]1 [—]1

**WORRY IS INTEREST
PAID ON TROUBLE
BEFORE IT FALLS DUE.
— W. R. INGE**
[.]1 [A]2 [B]2 [D]2 [E]6 [F]2 [I]4 [L]3
[N]2 [O]4 [P]1 [R]5 [S]3 [T]4 [U]2 [W]1 [Y]1
[.]2 [E]1 [G]1 [I]1 [N]1 [R]1 [W]1 [—]1

**UNLESS YOU LIKE
REELING IN WOE,
CAST YOUR CARES
ON THE FISHER OF MEN.**
[,]1 [.]1 [A]2 [C]2 [E]9 [F]2 [G]1 [H]2 [I]4 [K]1
[L]3 [M]1 [N]5 [O]5 [R]4 [S]5 [T]2 [U]3 [W]1 [Y]2

**LEAVE TOMORROW'S
TROUBLE TO TOMORROW'S
STRENGTH. — ANONYMOUS**
[']2 [.]1 [A]1 [B]1 [E]4 [G]1 [H]1 [L]2
[M]2 [N]1 [O]8 [R]6 [S]3 [T]6 [U]1 [V]1 [W]2
[A]1 [M]1 [N]2 [O]2 [S]1 [U]1 [Y]1 [—]1

**I WANT YOU TO BE FREE
FROM THE WORRIES
OF THIS WORLD.
— 2 CORINTHIANS 7:32**
[—]1 [.]1 [2]2 [3]1 [7]1 [:]1 [A]2 [B]1 [C]1 [D]1 [E]5 [F]3
[H]3 [I]5 [L]1 [M]1 [N]3 [O]7 [R]6 [S]3 [T]5 [U]1 [W]3 [Y]1

**THE LORD IS MY LIGHT
AND MY SALVATION;
WHOM SHALL I FEAR?
— PSALMS 27:1**
[—]1 [1]1 [2]2 [7]1 [:]1 [;]1 [?]1 [A]6 [D]2 [E]2 [F]1 [G]1
[H]4 [I]4 [L]6 [M]4 [N]2 [O]3 [P]1 [R]2 [S]4 [T]3 [V]1 [W]1 [Y]2

**LUCIFER LIKES
TO PLAY THE
SHAME GAME.**
[.]1 [A]3 [C]1 [E]5 [F]1 [G]1 [H]2 [I]2 [K]1
[L]3 [M]2 [O]1 [P]1 [R]1 [S]2 [T]2 [U]1 [Y]1

**TRUST AND WORRY
DO NOT GO TOGETHER.
— H. W. SMITH**
[.]1 [A]1 [D]2 [E]2 [G]2 [H]1 [N]2
[O]5 [R]4 [S]1 [T]5 [U]1 [W]1 [Y]1
[.]2 [H]2 [I]1 [M]1 [S]1 [T]1 [W]1 [—]1

EVERY PROBLEM HAS
IN IT THE SEEDS
OF ITS OWN SOLUTION.
— NORMAN VINCENT PEALE

    [.]1 [A]1 [B]1 [D]1 [E]6 [F]1 [H]2 [I]4 [L]2 [M]1
    [N]3 [O]5 [P]1 [R]2 [S]5 [T]4 [U]1 [V]1 [W]1 [Y]1
    [A]2 [C]1 [E]3 [I]1 [L]1 [M]1 [N]4 [O]1 [P]1 [R]1 [T]1 [V]1 [—]1

WORRY TAKES AS MUCH
TIME AS WORK
AND PAYS LESS.
— ANONYMOUS

    [.]1 [A]5 [C]1 [D]1 [E]3 [H]1 [I]1 [K]2 [L]1
    [M]2 [N]1 [O]2 [P]1 [R]3 [S]6 [T]2 [U]1 [W]2 [Y]2
    [A]1 [M]1 [N]2 [O]2 [S]1 [U]1 [Y]1 [—]1

BORROWING TROUBLE
FROM THE FUTURE
DOES NOT DEPLETE
THE SUPPLY.
(*Wings of Silver*)

    [.]1 [B]2 [D]2 [E]8 [F]2 [G]1 [H]2 [I]1 [L]3
    [M]1 [N]2 [O]6 [P]3 [R]5 [S]2 [T]6 [U]4 [W]1 [Y]1

Character References

Testaments to true grit

**NOTHING SHOWS
A MAN'S CHARACTER
MORE THAN WHAT HE
LAUGHS AT. — GOETHE**
[']1 [.]1 [A]8 [C]2 [E]3 [G]2 [H]7 [I]1
[L]1 [M]2 [N]4 [O]3 [R]3 [S]4 [T]5 [U]1 [W]2
[E]2 [G]1 [H]1 [O]1 [T]1 [—]1

**IT'S NOT WHO
BUT WHOSE
YOU ARE.**
[']1 [.]1 [A]1 [B]1 [E]2 [H]2 [I]1
[N]1 [O]4 [R]1 [S]2 [T]3 [U]2 [W]2 [Y]1

**FEW MEN HAVE VIRTUE
TO WITHSTAND THE
HIGHEST BIDDER.
— GEORGE WASHINGTON**
[.]1 [A]2 [B]1 [D]3 [E]7 [F]1 [G]1 [H]5 [I]4
[M]1 [N]2 [O]1 [R]2 [S]2 [T]6 [U]1 [V]2 [W]2
[A]1 [E]2 [G]3 [H]1 [I]1 [N]2 [O]2 [R]1 [S]1 [T]1 [W]1 [—]1

**NEARLY EVERYONE CAN
HANDLE BAD LUCK. IT'S
GOOD LUCK THAT REALLY
TESTS OUR CHARACTER.**
[']1 [.]2 [A]8 [B]1 [C]5 [D]3 [E]8 [G]1 [H]3 [I]1
[K]2 [L]6 [N]4 [O]4 [R]6 [S]3 [T]6 [U]3 [V]1 [Y]3

**YOU CAN ONLY LIVE ONCE —
BUT IF YOU DO IT RIGHT,
ONCE IS ENOUGH.**

    [,]1 [—]1 [.]1 [A]1 [B]1 [C]3 [D]1 [E]4 [F]1 [G]2
    [H]2 [I]5 [L]2 [N]5 [O]7 [R]1 [S]1 [T]3 [U]4 [V]1 [Y]3

**NOTHING IS SO STRONG
AS GENTLENESS.
NOTHING IS SO GENTLE
AS REAL STRENGTH.**
(*Wings of Silver*)

    [.]2 [A]3 [E]7 [G]6 [H]3 [I]4
    [L]3 [N]9 [O]5 [R]3 [S]10 [T]7

**NO REVENGE IS MORE
HONORABLE THAN
THE ONE NOT TAKEN.
— SPANISH PROVERB**

    [.]1 [A]3 [B]1 [E]8 [G]1 [H]3 [I]1 [K]1
    [L]1 [M]1 [N]7 [O]6 [R]3 [S]1 [T]4 [V]1
    [A]1 [B]1 [E]1 [H]1 [I]1 [N]1 [O]1 [P]2 [R]2 [S]2 [V]1 [—]1

**WE'RE NEVER MORE ON
TRIAL THAN IN TIMES
OF GOOD FORTUNE.
— REVISED LEW WALLACE**

    [']1 [.]1 [A]2 [D]1 [E]7 [F]2 [G]1 [H]1 [I]3
    [L]1 [M]2 [N]5 [O]6 [R]5 [S]1 [T]4 [U]1 [V]1 [W]1
    [A]2 [C]1 [D]1 [E]4 [I]1 [L]3 [R]1 [S]1 [V]1 [W]2 [—]1

**WHEN YOU STAND
FOR MORE, YOU
FALL FOR LESS.**

[,]1 [.]1 [A]2 [D]1 [E]3 [F]3 [H]1 [L]3
[M]1 [N]2 [O]5 [R]3 [S]3 [T]1 [U]2 [W]1 [Y]2

TRUE LOVE WAITS.

[.]1 [A]1 [E]2 [I]1 [L]1 [O]1
[R]1 [S]1 [T]2 [U]1 [V]1 [W]1

**WHEN YOU HIT
ROCK BOTTOM, YOU'VE
STILL GOT SOMETHING
TO BUILD ON.**

[']1 [,]1 [.]1 [B]2 [C]1 [D]1 [E]3 [G]2 [H]3 [I]4 [K]1
[L]3 [M]2 [N]3 [O]9 [R]1 [S]2 [T]7 [U]3 [V]1 [W]1 [Y]2

**YOU DON'T HAVE
TO RISE IN THE
WORLD TO RISE
TO THE OCCASION.**

[']1 [.]1 [A]2 [C]2 [D]2 [E]5 [H]3 [I]4 [L]1
[N]3 [O]8 [R]3 [S]3 [T]6 [U]1 [V]1 [W]1 [Y]1

**IT'S EASIER TO FIGHT
FOR ONE'S PRINCIPLES
THAN IT IS TO
LIVE UP TO THEM.**
(*Wings of Silver*)

[']2 [.]1 [A]2 [C]1 [E]6 [F]2 [G]1 [H]3 [I]8
[L]2 [M]1 [N]3 [O]5 [P]3 [R]3 [S]5 [T]8 [U]1 [V]1

111

GREAT MEN
ARE NOT
ALWAYS WISE.
— JOB 32:9

[—]1 [.]1 [2]1 [3]1 [9]1 [:]1 [A]4 [B]1 [E]4 [G]1
[I]1 [J]1 [L]1 [M]1 [N]2 [O]2 [R]2 [S]2 [T]2 [W]2 [Y]1

On Bended Knee

And everyone said "Amen"

BEFORE WORSE
COMES TO WORST,
YOU'VE ALWAYS
GOT A PRAYER.
[']1 [,]1 [.]1 [A]4 [B]1 [C]1 [E]6 [F]1 [G]1 [L]1
[M]1 [O]7 [P]1 [R]5 [S]4 [T]3 [U]1 [V]1 [W]3 [Y]3

WHEN FEAR
PREYS ON YOU,
PRAY ON IT.
[,]1 [.]1 [A]2 [E]3 [F]1 [H]1 [I]1 [N]3
[O]3 [P]2 [R]3 [S]1 [T]1 [U]1 [W]1 [Y]3

NOBODY DOESN'T
HAVE A PRAYER.
[']1 [.]1 [A]3 [B]1 [D]2 [E]3 [H]1
[N]2 [O]3 [P]1 [R]2 [S]1 [T]1 [V]1 [Y]2

HOW IS PRAYER
LIKE A PIANO?
YOU HAVE TO
PRACTICE DAILY.
[.]1 [?]1 [A]6 [C]2 [D]1 [E]4 [H]2 [I]5 [K]1 [L]2
[N]1 [O]4 [P]3 [R]3 [S]1 [T]2 [U]1 [V]1 [W]1 [Y]3

DAILY PRAYERS
WILL DIMINISH
YOUR CARES.
— BETTY MILLS
[.]1 [A]3 [C]1 [D]2 [E]2 [H]1 [I]5 [L]3
[M]1 [N]1 [O]1 [P]1 [R]4 [S]3 [U]1 [W]1 [Y]3
[B]1 [E]1 [I]1 [L]2 [M]1 [S]1 [T]2 [Y]1 [—]1

GIVE YOUR
TROUBLES TO GOD.
HE'LL BE UP
ALL NIGHT ANYWAY.
(*Wings of Silver*)
[']1 [.]2 [A]3 [B]2 [D]1 [E]4 [G]3 [H]2 [I]2 [L]5
[N]2 [O]4 [P]1 [R]2 [S]1 [T]3 [U]3 [V]1 [W]1 [Y]3

ASK TO DO
HIS WILL AND YOU'LL
ALWAYS GET WHAT
YOU PRAY FOR.
[']1 [.]1 [A]6 [D]2 [E]1 [F]1 [G]1 [H]2 [I]2 [K]1
[L]5 [N]1 [O]5 [P]1 [R]2 [S]3 [T]3 [U]2 [W]3 [Y]4

NO MAN EVER
PRAYED HEARTILY
WITHOUT LEARNING
SOMETHING. — EMERSON
[.]1 [A]4 [D]1 [E]6 [G]2 [H]3 [I]4 [L]2 [M]2
[N]5 [O]3 [P]1 [R]4 [S]1 [T]4 [U]1 [V]1 [W]1 [Y]2
[E]2 [M]1 [N]1 [O]1 [R]1 [S]1 [—]1

**GOD HEARS NO
MORE THAN THE
HEART SPEAKS.
—THOMAS BROOKS**

[.]1 [A]4 [D]1 [E]5 [G]1 [H]4 [K]1
[M]1 [N]2 [O]3 [P]1 [R]3 [S]3 [T]3
[A]1 [B]1 [H]1 [K]1 [M]1 [O]3 [R]1 [S]2 [T]1 [—]1

**IF YOU'RE BESIDE
YOURSELF, NOW
YOU CAN PRAY
TWICE AS HARD.**

[']1 [,]1 [.]1 [A]4 [B]1 [C]2 [D]2 [E]5 [F]2 [H]1
[I]3 [L]1 [N]2 [O]4 [P]1 [R]4 [S]3 [T]1 [U]3 [W]2 [Y]4

**WHY PRAY WHEN
YOU CAN WORRY?
— ANONYMOUS**

[?]1 [A]2 [C]1 [E]1 [H]2 [N]2 [O]2 [P]1 [R]3 [U]1 [W]3 [Y]4
[A]1 [M]1 [N]2 [O]2 [S]1 [U]1 [Y]1 [—]1

**WHEN LIFTING
HEAVY LOADS,
BEND AT THE KNEES.**

[,]1 [.]1 [A]3 [B]1 [D]2 [E]6 [F]1 [G]1 [H]3
[I]2 [K]1 [L]2 [N]4 [O]1 [S]2 [T]3 [V]1 [W]1 [Y]1

**PRAY FOR
NOTHING LESS
THAN TO LOVE
JESUS MORE.**

[.]1 [A]2 [E]4 [F]1 [G]1 [H]2 [I]1 [J]1 [L]2
[M]1 [N]3 [O]5 [P]1 [R]3 [S]4 [T]3 [U]1 [V]1 [Y]1

LIFE'S A TEST.
PRAY HARD.
['] 1 [.]2 [A]3 [D]1 [E]2 [F]1 [H]1
[I]1 [L]1 [P]1 [R]2 [S]2 [T]2 [Y]1

PRAYER IS
A SURVIVAL SKILL.
[.]1 [A]3 [E]1 [I]3 [K]1 [L]3
[P]1 [R]3 [S]3 [U]1 [V]2 [Y]1

LIFE IS FRAGILE.
HANDLE WITH PRAYER.
[.]2 [A]3 [D]1 [E]4 [F]2 [G]1 [H]2 [I]4
[L]3 [N]1 [P]1 [R]3 [S]1 [T]1 [W]1 [Y]1

WHEN YOU CALL
ON GOD OFTEN,
HE HEARS
A FAMILIAR RING.
[,]1 [.]1 [A]5 [C]1 [D]1 [E]4 [F]2 [G]2 [H]3 [I]3
[L]3 [M]1 [N]4 [O]4 [R]3 [S]1 [T]1 [U]1 [W]1 [Y]1

WHEN YOU'RE AT
THE END OF YOUR ROPE,
IT'S TIME TO GET
GOD ON THE LINE.
[']2 [,]1 [.]1 [A]1 [D]2 [E]9 [F]1 [G]2 [H]3 [I]3
[L]1 [M]1 [N]4 [O]7 [P]1 [R]3 [S]1 [T]7 [U]2 [W]1 [Y]2

PRAY FOR KEEPS.
[.]1 [A]1 [E]2 [F]1 [K]1
[O]1 [P]2 [R]2 [S]1 [Y]1

116

IT'S HARD TO
LOOK DOWN ON
SOMEONE WHEN YOU'RE
ON YOUR KNEES.

[']2 [.]1 [A]1 [D]2 [E]6 [H]2 [I]1 [K]2 [L]1
[M]1 [N]6 [O]10 [R]3 [S]3 [T]2 [U]2 [W]2 [Y]2

IF YOU'RE DOWN
ON YOURSELF,
TRY GETTING UP
ON YOUR KNEES.

[']1 [,]1 [.]1 [D]1 [E]5 [F]2 [G]2 [I]2 [K]1 [L]1
[N]5 [O]6 [P]1 [R]4 [S]2 [T]3 [U]4 [W]1 [Y]4

THE BEST WAY UP
IS DOWN ON
YOUR KNEES.

[.]1 [A]1 [B]1 [D]1 [E]4 [H]1 [I]1 [K]1
[N]3 [O]3 [P]1 [R]1 [S]3 [T]2 [U]2 [W]2 [Y]2

HE'S THE ANSWER
TO ALL YOUR PRAYERS.

[']1 [.]1 [A]3 [E]4 [H]2 [L]2 [N]1
[O]2 [P]1 [R]4 [S]3 [T]2 [U]1 [W]1 [Y]2

OUR PRAYERS ARE WITH
ALL WHO PASS THIS WAY.

[.]1 [A]5 [E]2 [H]3 [I]2 [L]2 [O]2
[P]2 [R]4 [S]4 [T]2 [U]1 [W]3 [Y]2

Peace Offerings

Lines of least resistance

**COME IN AND PICK
UP THE PEACES:
PEACE OF GOD,
PEACE OF MIND.**

[,]1 [.]1 [:]1 [A]4 [C]5 [D]3 [E]8 [F]2 [G]1
[H]1 [I]3 [K]1 [M]2 [N]3 [O]4 [P]5 [S]1 [T]1 [U]1

**DON'T LET THE PEACE
THAT PASSES
UNDERSTANDING
PASS YOU BY.**

[']1 [.]1 [A]5 [B]1 [C]1 [D]3 [E]6 [G]1 [H]2
[I]1 [L]1 [N]4 [O]2 [P]3 [R]1 [S]6 [T]6 [U]2 [Y]2

**PEACE MAY PASS
UNDERSTANDING, BUT IT
TAILGATES FAITH.**

[,]1 [.]1 [A]7 [B]1 [C]1 [D]2 [E]4 [F]1 [G]2 [H]1
[I]4 [L]1 [M]1 [N]3 [P]2 [R]1 [S]4 [T]6 [U]2 [Y]1

**AS MUCH AS IS POSSIBLE,
LIVE PEACEABLY
WITH ALL MEN.
— ROMANS 12:18**

[,]1 [—]1 [.]1 [1]2 [2]1 [8]1 [:]1 [A]6 [B]2 [C]2 [E]5 [H]2
[I]4 [L]5 [M]3 [N]2 [O]2 [P]2 [R]1 [S]6 [T]1 [U]1 [V]1 [W]1 [Y]1

**PASS ON THE PEACE
THAT PASSES
UNDERSTANDING.**

[.]1 [A]5 [C]1 [D]2 [E]5 [G]1 [H]2
[I]1 [N]4 [O]1 [P]3 [R]1 [S]6 [T]4 [U]1

**GOD HAS CALLED
US TO PEACE.
— 1 CORINTHIANS 7:15**

[—]1 [.]1 [1]2 [5]1 [7]1 [:]1 [A]4 [C]3 [D]2 [E]3
[G]1 [H]2 [I]2 [L]2 [N]2 [O]3 [P]1 [R]1 [S]3 [T]2 [U]1

**GOT MILK.
GOT PEACE?**

[.]1 [?]1 [A]1 [C]1 [E]2 [G]2
[I]1 [K]1 [L]1 [M]1 [O]2 [P]1 [T]2

**COME IN CONTRITE.
GO IN PEACE.**

[.]2 [A]1 [C]3 [E]4 [G]1 [I]3
[M]1 [N]3 [O]3 [P]1 [R]1 [T]2

Signs Of Salvation

Redeemingly good news from the gospel

ALL WHO'VE SINNED,
CHRIST CAN MEND.
[']1 [,]1 [.]1 [A]2 [C]2 [D]2 [E]3 [H]2 [I]2
[L]2 [M]1 [N]4 [O]1 [R]1 [S]2 [T]1 [V]1 [W]1

IN A COMPLICATED
WORLD, WE SIMPLY
NEED A SAVIOR.
[,]1 [.]1 [A]4 [C]2 [D]3 [E]4 [I]4 [L]3 [M]2
[N]2 [O]3 [P]2 [R]2 [S]2 [T]1 [V]1 [W]2 [Y]1

JOHN 3:16.
JUST SAY THE WORD.
[.]2 [1]1 [3]1 [6]1 [:]1 [A]1 [D]1 [E]1 [H]2
[J]2 [N]1 [O]2 [R]1 [S]2 [T]2 [U]1 [W]1 [Y]1

SOULS RECYCLED HERE.
[.]1 [C]2 [D]1 [E]4 [H]1
[L]2 [O]1 [R]2 [S]2 [U]1 [Y]1

OUR JOB ISN'T TO
REDEEM SOCIETY
BUT THE PEOPLE IN IT.
[']1 [.]1 [B]2 [C]1 [D]1 [E]7 [H]1 [I]4 [J]1
[L]1 [M]1 [N]2 [O]5 [P]2 [R]2 [S]2 [T]6 [U]2 [Y]1

**IF ONE CAN
BE REDEEMED,
SO CAN WE ALL.**
    [,]1 [.]1 [A]3 [B]1 [C]2 [D]2 [E]7 [F]1
    [I]1 [L]2 [M]1 [N]3 [O]2 [R]1 [S]1 [W]1

**THREE DAYS IN THE
BOWELS OF A BIG FISH
MAY STINK, BUT IT
SURE BEATS DROWNING.**
    [,]1 [.]1 [A]4 [B]4 [D]2 [E]6 [F]2 [G]2 [H]3 [I]6
    [K]1 [L]1 [M]1 [N]4 [O]3 [R]3 [S]6 [T]6 [U]2 [W]2 [Y]2

**WITH A GREAT
PRICE WE WERE
BOUGHT — NOT PAWNED.**
    [—]1 [.]1 [A]3 [B]1 [C]1 [D]1 [E]6 [G]2
    [H]2 [I]2 [N]2 [O]2 [P]2 [R]3 [T]4 [U]1 [W]4

**REPENT.
IT'LL DO
YOUR HEART GOOD.**
    [']1 [.]2 [A]1 [D]2 [E]3 [G]1 [H]1 [I]1
    [L]2 [N]1 [O]4 [P]1 [R]3 [T]3 [U]1 [Y]1

**JESUS IS A
LIFE SAVIOR.**
    [.]1 [A]2 [E]2 [F]1 [I]3 [J]1
    [L]1 [O]1 [R]1 [S]4 [U]1 [V]1

**REPENTANCE IS
AN ABOUT-FACE,
NOT ABOUT
SAVING FACE.**
[,]1 [-]1 [.]1 [A]7 [B]2 [C]3 [E]5 [F]2 [G]1
[I]2 [N]5 [O]3 [P]1 [R]1 [S]2 [T]4 [U]2 [V]1

**MADE CLEAN
BY HIS BLOOD,
KEPT CLEAN
BY HIS WORD.**
[,]1 [.]1 [A]3 [B]3 [C]2 [D]3 [E]4 [H]2 [I]2 [K]1
[L]3 [M]1 [N]2 [O]3 [P]1 [R]1 [S]2 [T]1 [W]1 [Y]2

**SOULS
REDEEMABLE
HERE.**
[.]1 [A]1 [B]1 [D]1 [E]6 [H]1
[L]2 [M]1 [O]1 [R]2 [S]2 [U]1

**JESUS WAS A MAN
AFTER OUR OWN HEART.**
[.]1 [A]5 [E]3 [F]1 [H]1 [J]1 [M]1
[N]2 [O]2 [R]3 [S]3 [T]2 [U]2 [W]2

**IF YOUR SINS
ARE FORGIVEN,
FUHGEDDABOUDEM!**
[!]1 [,]1 [A]2 [B]1 [D]3 [E]4 [F]3 [G]2 [H]1
[I]3 [M]1 [N]2 [O]3 [R]3 [S]2 [U]3 [V]1 [Y]1

Ten For Tolerance

*How to make a world of difference
in a world of differences*

**WOULDN'T IT BE NICE
IF WE COULD FIND
OTHER THINGS AS
EASILY AS WE FIND FAULT?**
(*Wings of Silver*)
['] 1 [?]1 [A]4 [B]1 [C]2 [D]4 [E]6 [F]4 [G]1 [H]2
[I]7 [L]4 [N]5 [O]3 [R]1 [S]4 [T]5 [U]3 [W]3 [Y]1

**JUDGMENT GETS
YOU NOWHERE.
— ANONYMOUS**
[.]1 [D]1 [E]4 [G]2 [H]1 [J]1 [M]1
[N]2 [O]2 [R]1 [S]1 [T]2 [U]2 [W]1 [Y]1
[A]1 [M]1 [N]2 [O]2 [S]1 [U]1 [Y]1 [—]1

**PROGRESS IS MADE
PEACE BY PEACE.**
[.]1 [A]3 [B]1 [C]2 [D]1 [E]6 [G]1
[I]1 [M]1 [O]1 [P]3 [R]2 [S]3 [Y]1

**PREJUDICE IS BEING
DOWN ON SOMETHING
YOU'RE NOT UP ON.
— ANONYMOUS**
['] 1 [.]1 [B]1 [C]1 [D]2 [E]5 [G]2 [H]1 [I]4 [J]1
[M]1 [N]6 [O]6 [P]2 [R]2 [S]2 [T]2 [U]3 [W]1 [Y]1
[A]1 [M]1 [N]2 [O]2 [S]1 [U]1 [Y]1 [—]1

ONE WHO TAKES DIGS
AT OTHERS MAY WELL
END UP IN THE HOLE.

[.]1 [A]3 [D]2 [E]7 [G]1 [H]4 [I]2 [K]1 [L]3
[M]1 [N]3 [O]4 [P]1 [R]1 [S]3 [T]4 [U]1 [W]2 [Y]1

IF YOU'VE AN AX TO
GRIND, BE PREPARED TO
BE THE GRINDSTONE.

[']1 [,]1 [.]1 [A]3 [B]2 [D]3 [E]7 [F]1 [G]2 [H]1
[I]3 [N]4 [O]4 [P]2 [R]4 [S]1 [T]4 [U]1 [V]1 [X]1 [Y]1

WE SHOULD INSTRUCT,
NOT ACCUSE.

[,]1 [.]1 [A]1 [C]3 [D]1 [E]2 [H]1 [I]1
[L]1 [N]2 [O]2 [R]1 [S]3 [T]3 [U]3 [W]1

WE BELIEVE IN THE
SEPARATION OF
CHURCH AND HATE.

[.]1 [A]4 [B]1 [C]2 [D]1 [E]7 [F]1 [H]4 [I]3
[L]1 [N]3 [O]2 [P]1 [R]2 [S]1 [T]3 [U]1 [V]1 [W]1

STRIVE NOT
FOR JUSTICE
BUT FOR MERCY.

[.]1 [B]1 [C]2 [E]3 [F]2 [I]2 [J]1 [M]1
[N]1 [O]3 [R]4 [S]2 [T]4 [U]2 [V]1 [Y]1

SOME SAINTS
MARCH TO A
DIFFERENT DRUMMER.
[.]1 [A]3 [C]1 [D]2 [E]4 [F]2 [H]1
[I]2 [M]4 [N]2 [O]2 [R]4 [S]3 [T]3 [U]1

The Bible Tells Us So

Strictly by the book

GOD LOVES
A CHEERFUL GIVER.
— 2 CORINTHIANS 9:6-7
[-]1 [—]1 [.]1 [2]1 [6]1 [7]1 [9]1 [:]1 [A]2 [C]2 [D]1 [E]4 [F]1
[G]2 [H]2 [I]3 [L]2 [N]2 [O]3 [R]3 [S]2 [T]1 [U]1 [V]2

TO WHOM MUCH IS GIVEN,
MUCH IS REQUIRED.
— LUKE 12:48
[,]1 [—]1 [.]1 [1]1 [2]1 [4]1 [8]1 [:]1 [C]2 [D]1 [E]4 [G]1 [H]3
[I]4 [K]1 [L]1 [M]3 [N]1 [O]2 [Q]1 [R]2 [S]2 [T]1 [U]4 [V]1 [W]1

IF YOU'RE A CHRISTIAN,
IT'S ALWAYS ALL
FOR THE BEST.
— ROMANS 8:28
[']2 [,]1 [—]1 [.]1 [2]1 [8]2 [:]1 [A]6 [B]1 [C]1 [E]3 [F]2
[H]2 [I]4 [L]3 [M]1 [N]2 [O]3 [R]4 [S]5 [T]4 [U]1 [W]1 [Y]2

EVEN CHRIST
HAD TO LEARN
OBEDIENCE.
— HEBREWS 5:8
[—]1 [.]1 [5]1 [8]1 [:]1 [A]2 [B]2 [C]2 [D]2 [E]8
[H]3 [I]2 [L]1 [N]3 [O]2 [R]3 [S]2 [T]2 [V]1 [W]1

129

DEAR FRIENDS,
LET US PRACTICE
LOVING EACH OTHER.
— 1 JOHN 4:7

[,]1 [—]1 [.]1 [1]1 [4]1 [7]1 [:]1 [A]3 [C]3 [D]2 [E]6 [F]1
[G]1 [H]3 [I]3 [J]1 [L]2 [N]3 [O]3 [P]1 [R]4 [S]2 [T]3 [U]1 [V]1

WEEPING MAY ENDURE
FOR A NIGHT, BUT JOY
COMES IN THE MORNING.
— PSALM 30:4-5

[,]1 [-]1 [—]1 [.]1 [0]1 [3]1 [4]1 [5]1 [:]1 [A]3 [B]1 [C]1 [D]1
[E]6 [F]1 [G]3 [H]2 [I]4 [J]1 [L]1 [M]4 [N]6 [O]4 [P]2 [R]3
[S]2 [T]3 [U]2 [W]1 [Y]2

NOT SEVEN
BUT SEVENTY
TIMES SEVEN.
— MATTHEW 18:22

[—]1 [.]1 [1]1 [2]2 [8]1 [:]1 [A]1 [B]1 [E]8 [H]1
[I]1 [M]2 [N]4 [O]1 [S]4 [T]6 [U]1 [V]3 [W]1 [Y]1

UNLESS YOU BECOME LIKE
A CHILD, YOU CANNOT
ENTER THE KINGDOM OF
HEAVEN. — MATTHEW 18:3

[,]1 [—]1 [.]1 [1]1 [3]1 [8]1 [:]1 [A]4 [B]1 [C]3 [D]2
[E]10 [F]1 [G]1 [H]4 [I]3 [K]2 [L]3 [M]3 [N]6 [O]6
[R]1 [S]2 [T]5 [U]3 [V]1 [W]1 [Y]2

A BIBLICAL RIDDLE
— JUDGES 14:14
[—]1 [1]2 [4]2 [:]1 [A]2 [B]2 [C]1 [D]3
[E]2 [G]1 [I]3 [J]1 [L]3 [R]1 [S]1 [U]1

GOT MILK AND HONEY?
— DEUTERONOMY 6:3, 18
[,]1 [—]1 [1]1 [3]1 [6]1 [8]1 [:]1 [?]1 [A]1 [D]2 [E]3
[G]1 [H]1 [I]1 [K]1 [L]1 [M]2 [N]3 [O]4 [R]1 [T]2 [U]1 [Y]2

SOMETIMES THE CROSS
WE MUST BEAR
ISN'T OUR OWN.
— MATTHEW 27:32
[']1 [—]1 [.]1 [2]2 [3]1 [7]1 [:]1 [A]2 [B]1 [C]1
[E]6 [H]2 [I]2 [M]4 [N]2 [O]4 [R]3 [S]6 [T]6 [U]2 [W]3

BE STILL
AND KNOW
THAT I AM GOD.
— PSALM 46:10
[—]1 [.]1 [0]1 [1]1 [4]1 [6]1 [:]1 [A]4 [B]1 [D]2 [E]1
[G]1 [H]1 [I]2 [K]1 [L]3 [M]2 [N]2 [O]2 [P]1 [S]2 [T]3 [W]1

WE HAVE NOT
BECAUSE WE ASK NOT.
— JAMES 4:2
[—]1 [.]1 [2]1 [4]1 [:]1 [A]4 [B]1 [C]1 [E]6 [H]1
[J]1 [K]1 [M]1 [N]2 [O]2 [S]3 [T]2 [U]1 [V]1 [W]2

The Christian Life

Talking the talk about walking the walk

**WHO WANTS TO BE
A CHRISTIANHEIR?**
[?]1 [A]3 [B]1 [C]1 [E]2 [H]3
[I]3 [N]2 [O]2 [R]2 [S]2 [T]3 [W]2

**WWJD?
WWUD?**
[?]2 [D]2
[J]1 [U]1 [W]4

**EXPECT GREAT THINGS
FROM GOD. ATTEMPT
GREAT THINGS FOR GOD.
— WILLIAM CAREY**
[.]2 [A]3 [C]1 [D]2 [E]5 [F]2 [G]6 [H]2
[I]2 [M]2 [N]2 [O]4 [P]2 [R]4 [S]2 [T]8 [X]1
[A]2 [C]1 [E]1 [I]2 [L]2 [M]1 [R]1 [W]1 [Y]1 [—]1

**THE EARLY CHURCH
WASN'T PERFECT,
EITHER — IT TOO HAD
PEOPLE IN IT.**
[']1 [,]1 [—]1 [.]1 [A]3 [C]3 [D]1 [E]8 [F]1 [H]5
[I]4 [L]2 [N]2 [O]3 [P]3 [R]4 [S]1 [T]7 [U]1 [W]1 [Y]1

THE LORD'S
LOVING KINDNESS
WILL NEVER LEAVE
YOU LONELY.

[']1 [.]1 [A]1 [D]2 [E]7 [G]1 [H]1 [I]3 [K]1
[L]7 [N]5 [O]4 [R]2 [S]3 [T]1 [U]1 [V]3 [W]1 [Y]2

GOOD VS. EVIL:
IT'S JUST YOUR
EVERYDAY
WRESTLEMANIA.

[']1 [.]2 [:]1 [A]3 [D]2 [E]5 [G]1 [I]3 [J]1 [L]2
[M]1 [N]1 [O]3 [R]3 [S]4 [T]3 [U]2 [V]3 [W]1 [Y]3

HIS RIGHTOUSNESS IS A
CROWN AND BREASTPLATE.
A DIVINE ENSEMBLE,
DON'T YOU THINK?

[']1 [,]1 [.]1 [?]1 [A]5 [B]2 [C]1 [D]3 [E]7 [G]1
[H]3 [I]6 [K]1 [L]2 [M]1 [N]7 [O]4 [P]1 [R]3
[S]7 [T]5 [U]2 [V]1 [W]1 [Y]1

LET US HELP EACH OTHER
TO SHOW LOVE AND DO
GOOD DEEDS.
— HEBREWS 10:24

[—]1 [.]1 [0]1 [1]1 [2]1 [4]1 [:]1 [A]2 [B]1 [C]1 [D]5 [E]9
[G]1 [H]5 [L]3 [N]1 [O]7 [P]1 [R]2 [S]4 [T]3 [U]1 [V]1 [W]2

BEAR FRUIT
— JOHN 15:16
(A NUT IS A
FRUIT, ISN'T IT?)
    [']1 [(]1 [)]1 [,]1 [—]1 [1]2 [5]1 [6]1 [:]1 [?]1 [A]3
    [B]1 [E]1 [F]2 [H]1 [I]5 [J]1 [N]3 [O]1 [R]3 [S]2 [T]5 [U]3

WE REAP WHAT WE SOW.
NO NEED TO FERTILIZE.
    [.]2 [A]2 [D]1 [E]7 [F]1 [H]1 [I]2 [L]1
    [N]2 [O]3 [P]1 [R]2 [S]1 [T]3 [W]4 [Z]1

TIME IS GOD'S GIFT
TO YOU. WHAT YOU DO
WITH YOUR TIME
IS YOUR GIFT TO GOD.
(God's Little Instruction Book)
    [']1 [.]2 [A]1 [D]3 [E]2 [F]2 [G]4 [H]2
    [I]7 [M]2 [O]9 [R]2 [S]3 [T]8 [U]4 [W]2 [Y]4

YOU EITHER
PRAYED TODAY
OR YOU DIDN'T.
    [']1 [.]1 [A]2 [D]4 [E]3 [H]1 [I]2
    [N]1 [O]4 [P]1 [R]3 [T]3 [U]2 [Y]4

I WOULD RATHER WALK
WITH GOD IN THE DARK
THAN GO ALONE IN THE
LIGHT. — M. G. BRAINARD
    [.]1 [A]5 [D]3 [E]4 [G]3 [H]6 [I]5
    [K]2 [L]4 [N]4 [O]4 [R]3 [T]6 [U]1 [W]3
    [.]2 [A]2 [B]1 [D]1 [G]1 [I]1 [M]1 [N]1 [R]2 [—]1

**EVERYONE'S A SLAVE
TO SOMETHING.
BUT WE GET TO CHOOSE
OUR MASTER.**
[']1 [.]2 [A]3 [B]1 [C]1 [E]9 [G]2 [H]2 [I]1 [L]1
[M]2 [N]2 [O]7 [R]3 [S]5 [T]6 [U]2 [V]2 [W]1 [Y]1

**WE SHOULDN'T BE SO
HEAVENLY MINDED THAT
WE'RE OF NO EARTHLY GOOD.
— ANONYMOUS**
[']2 [.]1 [A]3 [B]1 [D]4 [E]8 [F]1 [G]1 [H]4 [I]1
[L]3 [M]1 [N]4 [O]6 [R]2 [S]2 [T]4 [U]1 [V]1 [W]2 [Y]2
[A]1 [M]1 [N]2 [O]2 [S]1 [U]1 [Y]1 [—]1

**WE CAN'T
TURN BACK THE CLOCK,
BUT WE CAN
CHANGE THE TIMES.**
[']1 [,]1 [.]1 [A]4 [B]2 [C]6 [E]6 [G]1 [H]3 [I]1
[K]2 [L]1 [M]1 [N]4 [O]1 [R]1 [S]1 [T]6 [U]2 [W]2

**HE WHO WANTS TO LEAD
THE ORCHESTRA MUST
TURN HIS BACK ON THE
CROWD. — MAX LUCADO**
[.]1 [A]4 [B]1 [C]3 [D]2 [E]5 [H]6 [I]1 [K]1
[L]1 [M]1 [N]3 [O]5 [R]4 [S]4 [T]7 [U]2 [W]3
[A]2 [C]1 [D]1 [L]1 [M]1 [O]1 [U]1 [X]1 [—]1

**DISCOVER WHAT IS
TRUE AND PRACTICE
WHAT IS GOOD.**
(*Wings of Silver*)
  [.]1 [A]4 [C]3 [D]3 [E]3 [G]1 [H]2 [I]4
  [N]1 [O]3 [P]1 [R]3 [S]3 [T]4 [U]1 [V]1 [W]2

**WHERE GOD HAS HIS
CHURCH, THE DEVIL
WILL HAVE HIS CHAPEL.
— SPANISH PROVERB**
  [,]1 [.]1 [A]3 [C]3 [D]2 [E]6 [G]1 [H]9 [I]4
  [L]4 [O]1 [P]1 [R]2 [S]3 [T]1 [U]1 [V]2 [W]2
  [A]1 [B]1 [E]1 [H]1 [I]1 [N]1 [O]1 [P]2 [R]2 [S]2 [V]1 [—]1

**SALVATION IS FREE,
BUT BEING A
CHRISTIAN IS COSTLY.**
(*Wings of Silver*)
  [,]1 [.]1 [A]4 [B]2 [C]2 [E]3 [F]1 [G]1 [H]1
  [I]6 [L]2 [N]3 [O]2 [R]2 [S]5 [T]4 [U]1 [V]1 [Y]1

**THOSE WHO'D RATHER
GIVE GOD A TIP THAN
A TITHE SHOULD
RECALL A TIP IS 15%**
  [%]1 [']1 [1]1 [5]1 [A]6 [C]1 [D]3 [E]5 [G]2 [H]6
  [I]5 [L]3 [N]1 [O]4 [P]2 [R]3 [S]3 [T]7 [U]1 [V]1 [W]1

**WHATEVER MAKES GOOD
CHRISTIANS MAKES
THEM GOOD CITIZENS.**
(*Wings of Silver*)
>   [.]1 [A]4 [C]2 [D]2 [E]6 [G]2 [H]3 [I]4 [K]2
>   [M]3 [N]2 [O]4 [R]2 [S]5 [T]4 [V]1 [W]1 [Z]1

**IT'S BETTER TO SUFFER
AN INJUSTICE THAN
TO COMMIT ONE.
— ANONYMOUS**
>   [']1 [.]1 [A]2 [B]1 [C]2 [E]5 [F]2 [H]1
>   [I]4 [J]1 [M]2 [N]4 [O]4 [R]2 [S]3 [T]8 [U]2
>   [A]1 [M]1 [N]2 [O]2 [S]1 [U]1 [Y]1 [—]1

**WHAT REALLY MATTERS
IS WHAT YOU DO WITH
WHAT YOU HAVE.
— SHIRLEY LORD**
>   [.]1 [A]6 [D]1 [E]3 [H]5 [I]2 [L]2 [M]1
>   [O]3 [R]2 [S]2 [T]6 [U]2 [V]1 [W]4 [Y]3
>   [D]1 [E]1 [H]1 [I]1 [L]2 [O]1 [R]2 [S]1 [Y]1 [—]1

**ONLY A LIFE LIVED
FOR OTHERS IS
WORTH LIVING.
— EINSTEIN**
>   [.]1 [A]1 [D]1 [E]3 [F]2 [G]1 [H]2 [I]5
>   [L]4 [N]2 [O]4 [R]3 [S]2 [T]2 [V]2 [W]1 [Y]1
>   [E]2 [I]2 [N]2 [S]1 [T]1 [—]1

**LIVE AS IF
EVERYTHING YOU DO
WILL EVENTUALLY BE
KNOWN. — HUGH PRATHER**
> [.]1 [A]2 [B]1 [D]1 [E]6 [F]1 [G]1 [H]1 [I]4 [K]1
> [L]5 [N]4 [O]3 [R]1 [S]1 [T]2 [U]2 [V]3 [W]2 [Y]3
> [A]1 [E]1 [G]1 [H]3 [P]1 [R]2 [T]1 [U]1 [—]1

**AUTHORITY CAN
BE DELEGATED, BUT
NOT RESPONSIBILITY.
— ANONYMOUS**
> [,]1 [.]1 [A]3 [B]3 [C]1 [D]2 [E]5 [G]1 [H]1
> [I]4 [L]2 [N]3 [O]3 [P]1 [R]2 [S]2 [T]6 [U]2 [Y]2
> [A]1 [M]1 [N]2 [O]2 [S]1 [U]1 [Y]1 [—]1

**WE ARE ALL PENCILS
IN THE HAND OF GOD.
— MOTHER TERESA**
> [.]1 [A]3 [C]1 [D]2 [E]4 [F]1 [G]1 [H]2
> [I]2 [L]3 [N]3 [O]2 [P]1 [R]1 [S]1 [T]1 [W]1
> [A]1 [E]3 [H]1 [M]1 [O]1 [R]2 [S]1 [T]2 [—]1

**SAINTS SHOULD BE THE
SALT OF THE EARTH,
NOT LEAVE A BAD TASTE
IN THE MOUTH.**
> [,]1 [.]1 [A]7 [B]2 [D]2 [E]8 [F]1 [H]6 [I]2
> [L]3 [M]1 [N]3 [O]4 [R]1 [S]5 [T]10 [U]2 [V]1

AS CHRISTIANS,
WE SHOULDN'T
BE HALF BAD.

[']1 [,]1 [.]1 [A]4 [B]2 [C]1 [D]2 [E]2 [F]1
[H]3 [I]2 [L]2 [N]2 [O]1 [R]1 [S]4 [T]2 [U]1 [W]1

STAND ON CEREMONY ONLY,
AND YOU'LL FALL
INTO A RUT.

[']1 [,]1 [.]1 [A]4 [C]1 [D]2 [E]2 [F]1 [I]1
[L]5 [M]1 [N]6 [O]5 [R]2 [S]1 [T]3 [U]2 [Y]3

OUR RELATIONSHIP WITH
GOD WILL INCLUDE
SADNESS, BUT IT SHOULDN'T
INCLUDE DESPAIR.

[']1 [,]1 [.]1 [A]3 [B]1 [C]2 [D]6 [E]5 [G]1 [H]3
[I]8 [L]6 [N]5 [O]4 [P]2 [R]3 [S]6 [T]5 [U]5 [W]2

HIS SHEEP
LIKE TO GATHER
IN A FLOCK TOGETHER.

[.]1 [A]2 [C]1 [E]6 [F]1 [G]2 [H]4 [I]3
[K]2 [L]2 [N]1 [O]3 [P]1 [R]2 [S]2 [T]4

LIFE'S A LEDGER.
ARE WE GIVING A GOOD
ACCOUNTING
OF OURSELVES?

[']1 [.]1 [?]1 [A]4 [C]2 [D]2 [E]7 [F]2 [G]5
[I]4 [L]3 [N]3 [O]5 [R]3 [S]3 [T]1 [U]2 [V]2 [W]1

**O LORD, MAKE US
STEPPING STONES,
NOT STUMBLING BLOCKS.**

[,]2 [.]1 [A]1 [B]2 [C]1 [D]1 [E]3 [G]2 [I]2
[K]2 [L]3 [M]2 [N]4 [O]5 [P]2 [R]1 [S]6 [T]4 [U]2

**IT'S OKAY TO HAVE
YOUR HEAD IN THE
CLOUDS IF THE REST OF
YOU IS WELL GROUNDED.**

[']1 [.]1 [A]3 [C]1 [D]4 [E]7 [F]2 [G]1 [H]4 [I]4
[K]1 [L]3 [N]2 [O]7 [R]3 [S]4 [T]5 [U]4 [V]1 [W]1 [Y]3

**ARE YOU A CHRISTIAN
OR A CHAMELEON?**

[?]1 [A]5 [C]2 [E]3 [H]2 [I]2 [L]1
[M]1 [N]2 [O]3 [R]3 [S]1 [T]1 [U]1 [Y]1

**PETER WENT
OVERBOARD
FOR THE LORD.
WHY CAN'T WE?**

[']1 [.]1 [?]1 [A]2 [B]1 [C]1 [D]2 [E]6 [F]1
[H]2 [L]1 [N]2 [O]4 [P]1 [R]5 [T]4 [V]1 [W]3 [Y]1

**WE'RE CALLED TO
BE CHILDREN OF THE
KING, NOT ROYAL PAINS.**

[']1 [,]1 [.]1 [A]3 [B]1 [C]2 [D]2 [E]6 [F]1 [G]1 [H]2
[I]3 [K]1 [L]4 [N]4 [O]4 [P]1 [R]3 [S]1 [T]3 [W]1 [Y]1

OUR OLD NATURE
WAS GRASPING; OUR
NEW NATURE IS GIVING.

[.]1 [;]1 [A]4 [D]1 [E]3 [G]4 [I]4 [L]1
[N]5 [O]3 [P]1 [R]5 [S]3 [T]2 [U]4 [V]1 [W]2

CIRCUMSTANCES CHANGE.
GOD DOESN'T.

[']1 [.]2 [A]2 [C]4 [D]2 [E]3 [G]2 [H]1
[I]1 [M]1 [N]3 [O]2 [R]1 [S]3 [T]2 [U]1

MATTHEW 11:30
— WHY GOD'S
WORK DOESN'T HURT.

[']2 [—]1 [.]1 [0]1 [1]2 [3]1 [:]1 [A]1 [D]2 [E]2 [G]1
[H]3 [K]1 [M]1 [N]1 [O]3 [R]2 [S]2 [T]4 [U]1 [W]3 [Y]1

WE SHOULDN'T
BE DISTRESSED
UNDER THE
CIRCUMSTANCES.

[']1 [.]1 [A]1 [B]1 [C]3 [D]4 [E]7 [H]2 [I]2
[L]1 [M]1 [N]3 [O]1 [R]3 [S]6 [T]4 [U]3 [W]1

CHRISTIANS ARE
HAPPY AS LAMBS.

[.]1 [A]5 [B]1 [C]1 [E]1 [H]2 [I]2
[L]1 [M]1 [N]1 [P]2 [R]2 [S]4 [T]1 [Y]1

**MAYBE YOU CAN'T
CHANGE THE WORLD,
BUT YOU CAN MAKE
A WORLD OF DIFFERENCE.**

[']1 [,]1 [.]1 [A]6 [B]2 [C]4 [D]3 [E]7 [F]3 [G]1 [H]2
[I]1 [K]1 [L]2 [M]2 [N]4 [O]5 [R]3 [T]3 [U]3 [W]2 [Y]3

**ARE YOU A CREDIT
TO YOUR MAKER?**

[?]1 [A]3 [C]1 [D]1 [E]3 [I]1
[K]1 [M]1 [O]3 [R]4 [T]2 [U]2 [Y]2

**JUST BECAUSE PEWS
COME IN ROWS DOESN'T
MEAN WE SHOULD PLANT
OURSELVES THERE.**

[']1 [.]1 [A]3 [B]1 [C]2 [D]2 [E]11 [H]2 [I]1 [J]1
[L]3 [M]2 [N]4 [O]5 [P]2 [R]3 [S]8 [T]4 [U]4 [V]1 [W]3

**THERE'S MORE TO
SELF-DENIAL THAN
MEETS THE "I."**

["]1 ["]1 [']1 [-]1 [.]1 [A]2 [D]1 [E]8 [F]1
[H]3 [I]2 [L]2 [M]2 [N]2 [O]2 [R]2 [S]3 [T]5

**IN THE SPIN-CYCLE
OF LIFE, GOD MAKES
OUR WORRIES CLING-FREE.**

[,]1 [-]2 [.]1 [A]1 [C]3 [D]1 [E]7 [F]3 [G]2 [H]1 [I]5
[K]1 [L]3 [M]1 [N]3 [O]4 [P]1 [R]4 [S]3 [T]1 [U]1 [W]1 [Y]1

**THERE'S NO MINIMUM
DAILY ALLOWANCE
ON THE FRUITS
OF THE SPIRIT.**

[']1 [.]1 [A]3 [C]1 [D]1 [E]5 [F]2 [H]3 [I]6 [L]3
[M]3 [N]4 [O]4 [P]1 [R]3 [S]3 [T]5 [U]2 [W]1 [Y]1

**GIVE LIFE
YOUR SUNDAY BEST.**

[.]1 [A]1 [B]1 [D]1 [E]3 [F]1 [G]1 [I]2
[L]1 [N]1 [O]1 [R]1 [S]2 [T]1 [U]2 [V]1 [Y]2

**FEED AN EGO,
STARVE A SPIRIT.**

[,]1 [.]1 [A]3 [D]1 [E]4 [F]1 [G]1
[I]2 [N]1 [O]1 [P]1 [R]2 [S]2 [T]2 [V]1

**THE EVENING OF
A WELL-SPENT LIFE
BRINGS ITS LAMP WITH IT.**

(Wings of Silver)

[-]1 [.]1 [A]2 [B]1 [E]6 [F]2 [G]2 [H]2 [I]6
[L]4 [M]1 [N]4 [O]1 [P]2 [R]1 [S]3 [T]5 [V]1 [W]2

**IF YOU LIVE
AFRAID OF LIFE,
YOU'LL LIVE
A FRAYED LIFE. — ANONYMOUS**

[']1 [,]1 [.]1 [A]4 [D]2 [E]5 [F]6
[I]6 [L]6 [O]3 [R]2 [U]2 [V]2 [Y]3
[A]1 [M]1 [N]2 [O]2 [S]1 [U]1 [Y]1 [—]1

144

Thus Saith Others

Sage advice from poets, philosophers,
theologians, and your everyday know-it-alls

A TRUE FRIEND NEVER
GETS IN YOUR WAY
UNLESS YOU HAPPEN
TO BE GOING DOWN.
— ARNOLD H. GLASGOW
[.]1 [A]3 [B]1 [D]2 [E]8 [F]1 [G]3 [H]1 [I]3 [L]1
[N]7 [O]5 [P]2 [R]4 [S]3 [T]3 [U]4 [V]1 [W]2 [Y]3
[.]1 [A]2 [D]1 [G]2 [H]1 [L]2 [N]1 [O]2 [R]1 [S]1 [W]1 [—]1

LIFE SHRINKS OR
EXPANDS IN PROPORTION
TO ONE'S COURAGE.
— ANAÏS NIN
[']1 [.]1 [A]2 [C]1 [D]1 [E]4 [F]1 [G]1 [H]1 [I]4
[K]1 [L]1 [N]5 [O]7 [P]3 [R]5 [S]4 [T]2 [U]1 [X]1
[A]2 [I]2 [N]3 [S]1 [—]1

FRIENDS DO NOT LIVE
IN HARMONY MERELY,
AS SOME SAY, BUT IN
MELODY. — THOREAU
[,]2 [.]1 [A]3 [B]1 [D]3 [E]6 [F]1 [H]1 [I]4
[L]3 [M]4 [N]5 [O]5 [R]3 [S]4 [T]2 [U]1 [V]1 [Y]4
[A]1 [E]1 [H]1 [O]1 [R]1 [T]1 [U]1 [—]1

EVERYTHING THAT
USED TO BE A SIN
IS NOW A DISEASE.
— BILL MAHER

    [.]1 [A]4 [B]1 [D]2 [E]6 [G]1 [H]2 [I]4
    [N]3 [O]2 [R]1 [S]5 [T]4 [U]1 [V]1 [W]1 [Y]1
    [A]1 [B]1 [E]1 [H]1 [I]1 [L]2 [M]1 [R]1 [—]1

TOMORROW IS THE
BUSIEST DAY
OF THE YEAR.
— SPANISH PROVERB

    [.]1 [A]2 [B]1 [D]1 [E]4 [F]1 [H]2 [I]2
    [M]1 [O]4 [R]3 [S]3 [T]4 [U]1 [W]1 [Y]2
    [A]1 [B]1 [E]1 [H]1 [I]1 [N]1 [O]1 [P]2 [R]2 [S]2 [V]1 [—]1

THE BEST WAY TO
CHEER YOURSELF UP
IS TO CHEER SOMEBODY
ELSE UP. — MARK TWAIN

    [.]1 [A]1 [B]2 [C]2 [D]1 [E]10 [F]1 [H]3 [I]1
    [L]2 [M]1 [O]5 [P]2 [R]3 [S]5 [T]4 [U]3 [W]1 [Y]3
    [A]2 [I]1 [K]1 [M]1 [N]1 [R]1 [T]1 [W]1 [—]1

IT'S EASY TO GET LOST
IN THOUGHT IF IT'S NOT
FAMILIAR TERRITORY.
— ANONYMOUS

    [']2 [.]1 [A]3 [E]3 [F]2 [G]2 [H]2 [I]7
    [L]2 [M]1 [N]2 [O]5 [R]4 [S]4 [T]10 [U]1 [Y]2
    [A]1 [M]1 [N]2 [O]2 [S]1 [U]1 [Y]1 [—]1

THERE'S AN OLD PROVERB
THAT SAYS JUST
ABOUT WHATEVER YOU
WANT IT TO. — ANONYMOUS
  [']1 [.]1 [A]6 [B]2 [D]1 [E]5 [H]3 [I]1 [J]1 [L]1
  [N]2 [O]5 [P]1 [R]4 [S]4 [T]9 [U]3 [V]2 [W]2 [Y]2
  [A]1 [M]1 [N]2 [O]2 [S]1 [U]1 [Y]1 [—]1

EVERYTHING COMES
TO HIM WHO HUSTLES
WHILE HE WAITS.
— EDISON
  [.]1 [A]1 [C]1 [E]6 [G]1 [H]6 [I]4 [L]2 [M]2
  [N]1 [O]3 [R]1 [S]4 [T]4 [U]1 [V]1 [W]3 [Y]1
  [D]1 [E]1 [I]1 [N]1 [O]1 [S]1 [—]1

THE PERSON WHO DOES
NOT MAKE A CHOICE
MAKES A CHOICE.
— JEWISH PROVERB
  [.]1 [A]4 [C]4 [D]1 [E]7 [H]4 [I]2 [K]2
  [M]2 [N]2 [O]6 [P]1 [R]1 [S]3 [T]2 [W]1
  [B]1 [E]2 [H]1 [I]1 [J]1 [O]1 [P]1 [R]2 [S]1 [V]1 [W]1 [—]1

DO EVERYTHING.
ONE THING MAY
TURN OUT RIGHT.
— HUMPHREY BOGART
  [.]2 [A]1 [D]1 [E]3 [G]3 [H]3 [I]3
  [M]1 [N]4 [O]3 [R]3 [T]5 [U]2 [V]1 [Y]2
  [A]1 [B]1 [E]1 [G]1 [H]2 [M]1 [O]1 [P]1 [R]2 [T]1 [U]1 [Y]1 [—]1

**FREEDOM LIES
IN BOLD ACTION.
— ROBERT FROST**
[.]1 [A]1 [B]1 [C]1 [D]2 [E]3 [F]1
[I]3 [L]2 [M]1 [N]2 [O]3 [R]1 [S]1 [T]1
[B]1 [E]1 [F]1 [O]2 [R]3 [S]1 [T]2 [—]1

**GOD DWELLS
WHEREVER MEN
LET HIM IN.
— MARTIN HUBER**
[.]1 [D]2 [E]6 [G]1 [H]2 [I]2 [L]3
[M]2 [N]2 [O]1 [R]2 [S]1 [T]1 [V]1 [W]2
[A]1 [B]2 [E]1 [I]1 [M]1 [N]1 [R]2 [T]1 [U]1 [—]1

**RESISTANCE
IS THE FIRST STEP
TO CHANGE.
— LOUISE HAY**
[.]1 [A]2 [C]2 [E]5 [F]1 [G]1 [H]2
[I]3 [N]2 [O]1 [P]1 [R]2 [S]5 [T]5
[A]1 [E]1 [H]1 [I]1 [L]1 [O]1 [S]1 [U]1 [Y]1 [—]1

**MAN IS BORN BROKEN.
HE LIVES BY MENDING.
THE GRACE OF GOD
IS GLUE. — EUGENE O'NEILL**
[.]3 [A]2 [B]3 [C]1 [D]2 [E]7 [F]1 [G]4 [H]2 [I]4
[K]1 [L]2 [M]2 [N]5 [O]4 [R]3 [S]3 [T]1 [U]1 [V]1 [Y]1
[']1 [E]4 [G]1 [I]1 [L]2 [N]2 [O]1 [U]1 [—]1

**WHAT YOU DISLIKE
IN ANOTHER, TAKE CARE
TO CORRECT IN YOURSELF.
— THOMAS SPRAT**

[,]1 [.]1 [A]4 [C]3 [D]1 [E]6 [F]1 [H]2 [I]4
[K]2 [L]2 [N]3 [O]5 [R]5 [S]2 [T]5 [U]2 [W]1 [Y]2
[A]2 [H]1 [M]1 [O]1 [P]1 [R]1 [S]2 [T]2 [—]1

**AS A MAN SPEAKS,
SO IS HE.
— PUBLILIUS SYRUS**

[,]1 [.]1 [A]4 [E]2 [H]1 [I]1 [K]1
[M]1 [N]1 [O]1 [P]1 [S]5
[B]1 [I]2 [L]2 [P]1 [R]1 [S]3 [U]3 [Y]1 [—]1

**ONE ON GOD'S SIDE
IS A MAJORITY.
— WENDELL PHILLIP**

[']1 [.]1 [A]2 [D]2 [E]2 [G]1 [I]3
[J]1 [M]1 [N]2 [O]4 [R]1 [S]3 [T]1 [Y]1
[D]1 [E]2 [H]1 [I]2 [L]4 [N]1 [P]2 [W]1 [—]1

**IF YOU ADD TO
THE TRUTH,
YOU SUBTRACT FROM IT.
— ANONYMOUS**

[,]1 [.]1 [A]2 [B]1 [C]1 [D]2 [E]1 [F]2
[H]2 [I]2 [M]1 [O]4 [R]3 [S]1 [T]7 [U]4 [Y]2
[A]1 [M]1 [N]2 [O]2 [S]1 [U]1 [Y]1 [—]1

LET GO AND LET GOD.
— 12 STEPS
[.]1 [1]1 [2]1 [A]1 [D]2 [E]3
[G]2 [L]2 [N]1 [O]2 [P]1 [S]2 [T]3

TRUST IN GOD
BUT TIE YOUR CAMEL.
— PERSIAN PROVERB
[.]1 [A]1 [B]1 [C]1 [D]1 [E]2 [G]1 [I]2
[L]1 [M]1 [N]1 [O]2 [R]2 [S]1 [T]4 [U]3 [Y]1
[A]1 [B]1 [E]2 [I]1 [N]1 [O]1 [P]2 [R]3 [S]1 [V]1 [—]1

THE HIGHEST POINT
A MAN CAN ATTAIN IS
... SACRED AWE.
— NIKOS KAZANTZAKIS
[.]4 [A]7 [C]2 [D]1 [E]4 [G]1 [H]3 [I]4
[M]1 [N]4 [O]1 [P]1 [R]1 [S]3 [T]5 [W]1
[A]3 [I]2 [K]3 [N]2 [O]1 [S]2 [T]1 [Z]2 [—]1

TRUTH EXISTS.
ONLY LIES
HAVE TO BE INVENTED.
— GEORGES BRAQUE
[.]2 [A]1 [B]1 [D]1 [E]6 [H]2 [I]3 [L]2
[N]3 [O]2 [R]1 [S]3 [T]5 [U]1 [V]2 [X]1 [Y]1
[A]1 [B]1 [E]3 [G]2 [O]1 [Q]1 [R]2 [S]1 [U]1 [—]1

A SMILE IS A CURVE
THAT CAN SET A LOT
OF THINGS STRAIGHT.
(*Wings of Silver*)
　　[.]1 [A]6 [C]2 [E]3 [F]1 [G]2 [H]3 [I]4
　　[L]2 [M]1 [N]2 [O]2 [R]2 [S]5 [T]7 [U]1 [V]1

A GOOD MEMORY IS FINE,
BUT THE ABILITY
TO FORGET IS THE TRUE
TEST OF GREATNESS.
(*Wings of Silver*)
　　[,]1 [.]1 [A]3 [B]2 [D]1 [E]9 [F]3 [G]3 [H]2
　　[I]5 [L]1 [M]2 [N]2 [O]6 [R]4 [S]5 [T]10 [U]2 [Y]2

GOD BRINGS COMFORT
TO THE TROUBLED AND
TROUBLE TO
THE COMFORTABLE.
(*Wings of Silver*)
　　[.]1 [A]2 [B]4 [C]2 [D]3 [E]5 [F]2 [G]2 [H]2
　　[I]1 [L]3 [M]2 [N]2 [O]9 [R]5 [S]1 [T]8 [U]2

THE GRASS IS GREENER
ON THE OTHER SIDE,
BUT IT'S JUST
AS HARD TO MOW.
(*Wings of Silver*)
　　[']1 [,]1 [.]1 [A]3 [B]1 [D]2 [E]7 [G]2 [H]4
　　[I]3 [J]1 [M]1 [N]2 [O]4 [R]5 [S]7 [T]7 [U]2 [W]1

GOD WILL NOT LOOK
YOU OVER FOR MEDALS
BUT FOR SCARS.
(*Wings of Silver*)
    [.]1 [A]2 [B]1 [C]1 [D]2 [E]2 [F]2 [G]1 [I]1 [K]1
    [L]4 [M]1 [N]1 [O]8 [R]4 [S]3 [T]2 [U]2 [V]1 [W]1 [Y]1

BETTER TO LIMP
ALL THE WAY TO HEAVEN
THAN NOT TO
GET THERE AT ALL.
(*Wings of Silver*)
    [.]1 [A]6 [B]1 [E]8 [G]1 [H]4 [I]1 [L]5
    [M]1 [N]3 [O]4 [P]1 [R]2 [T]11 [V]1 [W]1 [Y]1

THEY ALSO SERVE
WHO ONLY STAND
AND WAIT.
— MILTON
    [.]1 [A]4 [D]2 [E]3 [H]2 [I]1 [L]2
    [N]3 [O]3 [R]1 [S]3 [T]3 [V]1 [W]2 [Y]2
    [I]1 [L]1 [M]1 [N]1 [O]1 [T]1 [—]1

BUILDING BOYS
IS EASIER THAN
MENDING MEN.
(*Wings of Silver*)
    [.]1 [A]2 [B]2 [D]2 [E]4 [G]2 [H]1 [I]5
    [L]1 [M]2 [N]5 [O]1 [R]1 [S]3 [T]1 [U]1 [Y]1

IF A MAN EMPTIES
HIS PURSE INTO
HIS HEAD, NO MAN
CAN TAKE IT FROM HIM.
(*Wings of Silver*)
> [,]1 [.]1 [A]6 [C]1 [D]1 [E]5 [F]2 [H]4 [I]7
> [K]1 [M]5 [N]5 [O]3 [P]2 [R]2 [S]4 [T]4 [U]1

THE BEST WAY
TO SUCCEED IS TO
ACT ON THE ADVICE
YOU GIVE OTHERS.
(*Wings of Silver*)
> [.]1 [A]3 [B]1 [C]4 [D]2 [E]8 [G]1 [H]3 [I]3
> [N]1 [O]5 [R]1 [S]4 [T]7 [U]2 [V]2 [W]1 [Y]2

THERE'S NOTHING
INDECENT ABOUT
THE NAKED TRUTH.
(*Wings of Silver*)
> [']1 [.]1 [A]2 [B]1 [C]1 [D]2 [E]6 [G]1
> [H]4 [I]2 [K]1 [N]5 [O]2 [R]2 [S]1 [T]7 [U]2

A SHIP IS SAFEST
IN DEEP WATER.
(*Wings of Silver*)
> [.]1 [A]3 [D]1 [E]4 [F]1 [H]1
> [I]3 [N]1 [P]2 [R]1 [S]4 [T]2 [W]1

BE SURE OF THIS:
YOU ARE DREADFULLY
LIKE OTHER PEOPLE.
(*Wings of Silver*)
[.]1 [:]1 [A]2 [B]1 [D]2 [E]8 [F]2 [H]2 [I]2
[K]1 [L]4 [O]4 [P]2 [R]4 [S]2 [T]2 [U]3 [Y]2

COMMIT A SIN TWICE
AND IT WILL SEEM
NO LONGER A SIN.
(*Wings of Silver*)
[.]1 [A]3 [C]2 [D]1 [E]4 [G]1 [I]6
[L]3 [M]3 [N]5 [O]3 [R]1 [S]3 [T]3 [W]2

THE FIRST STEP
IN MAKING A DREAM
COME TRUE
IS TO WAKE UP.
(*Wings of Silver*)
[.]1 [A]4 [C]1 [D]1 [E]6 [F]1 [G]1 [H]1 [I]4
[K]2 [M]3 [N]2 [O]2 [P]2 [R]3 [S]3 [T]5 [U]2 [W]1

GOSSIP IS PUTTING
TWO AND TWO TOGETHER
AND MAKING FIVE.
(*Wings of Silver*)
[.]1 [A]3 [D]2 [E]3 [F]1 [G]4 [H]1 [I]5 [K]1
[M]1 [N]4 [O]4 [P]2 [R]1 [S]3 [T]6 [U]1 [V]1 [W]2

EVERY DAY IS A
GIFT FROM GOD.
THAT'S WHY IT'S CALLED
THE PRESENT. — ANONYMOUS

[']2 [.]2 [A]4 [C]1 [D]3 [E]6 [F]2 [G]2 [H]3 [I]3
[L]2 [M]1 [N]1 [O]2 [P]1 [R]3 [S]4 [T]6 [V]1 [W]1 [Y]3
[A]1 [M]1 [N]2 [O]2 [S]1 [U]1 [Y]1 [—]1

Timely Ruminations
For Special Occasions

To every season there is a marquee

New Year

**LOOK BACKWARD IN
THANKSGIVING,
LOOK FORWARD IN HOPE.**
[,]1 [.]1 [A]4 [B]1 [C]1 [D]2 [E]1 [F]1 [G]2 [H]2
[I]4 [K]4 [L]2 [N]4 [O]6 [P]1 [R]3 [S]1 [T]1 [V]1 [W]2

Martin Luther King, Jr. Day

**INJUSTICE ANYWHERE
IS A THREAT TO
JUSTICE EVERYWHERE.
— M. L. KING, JR.**
[.]1 [A]3 [C]2 [E]9 [H]3 [I]4 [J]2 [N]2
[O]1 [R]4 [S]3 [T]5 [U]2 [V]1 [W]2 [Y]2
[,]1 [.]3 [G]1 [I]1 [J]1 [K]1 [L]1 [M]1 [N]1 [R]1 [—]1

**LIFE IS MORE
WORTH LIVING WHEN
WE FIND SOMETHING
WORTH DYING FOR.
— REVISED M. L. KING, JR.**
[.]1 [D]2 [E]5 [F]3 [G]3 [H]4 [I]7 [L]2
[M]2 [N]5 [O]5 [R]4 [S]2 [T]3 [V]1 [W]4 [Y]1
[,]1 [.]3 [D]1 [E]2 [G]1 [I]2 [J]1 [K]1 [L]1
[M]1 [N]1 [R]2 [S]1 [V]1 [—]1

Valentine's Day

**MAY YOU
AND YOUR LOVE
PARTY HEARTILY.**
> [.]1 [A]4 [D]1 [E]2 [H]1 [I]1 [L]2 [M]1
> [N]1 [O]3 [P]1 [R]3 [T]2 [U]2 [V]1 [Y]5

**LOVE IS ...
THE AMEN OF
THE UNIVERSE.
— NOVALIS**
> [.]4 [A]1 [E]6 [F]1 [H]2 [I]2 [L]1
> [M]1 [N]2 [O]2 [R]1 [S]2 [T]2 [U]1 [V]2
> [A]1 [I]1 [L]1 [N]1 [O]1 [S]1 [V]1 [—]1

**LOVE IS LIKE A BOX
OF CHOCOLATES —
FULL OF
SWEET SURPRISES.**
> [—]1 [.]1 [A]2 [B]1 [C]2 [E]6 [F]3 [H]1 [I]3 [K]1
> [L]5 [O]6 [P]1 [R]2 [S]6 [T]2 [U]2 [V]1 [W]1 [X]1

Spring

**IT'S A GREAT DAY.
LET'S HAVE CHURCH!**
> [!]1 [']2 [.]1 [A]4 [C]2 [D]1 [E]3 [G]1
> [H]3 [I]1 [L]1 [R]2 [S]2 [T]3 [U]1 [V]1 [Y]1

IT'S PLANTING TIME!
COME IN FOR
YOUR MUSTARD SEEDS
OF FAITH.
[!]1 [']1 [.]1 [A]3 [C]1 [D]2 [E]4 [F]3 [G]1 [H]1
[I]5 [L]1 [M]3 [N]3 [O]4 [P]1 [R]3 [S]4 [T]5 [U]2 [Y]1

Passion Week

MUST JESUS
BEAR THE CROSS
ALONE?
[?]1 [A]2 [B]1 [C]1 [E]4 [H]1 [J]1
[L]1 [M]1 [N]1 [O]2 [R]2 [S]5 [T]2 [U]2

Easter

ENTER
THE HOUSE OF
THE RISEN SON.
[.]1 [E]6 [F]1 [H]3 [I]1
[N]3 [O]3 [R]2 [S]3 [T]3 [U]1

THE EARTH
IS ALIVE
WITH EASTER!
[!]1 [A]3 [E]5 [H]3 [I]3 [L]1
[R]2 [S]2 [T]4 [V]1 [W]1

THE RISEN SON
WAS GOD'S
BRIGHT IDEA.
[']1 [.]1 [A]2 [B]1 [D]2 [E]3 [G]2
[H]2 [I]3 [N]2 [O]2 [R]2 [S]4 [T]2 [W]1

THE STONE COULDN'T
STAY WHEN THE
ROCK OF AGES
SAID ROLL.
[']1 [.]1 [A]3 [C]2 [D]2 [E]5 [F]1 [G]1 [H]3 [I]1
[K]1 [L]3 [N]3 [O]5 [R]2 [S]4 [T]5 [U]1 [W]1 [Y]1

HOSANNA TO
THE KING OF KINGS.
[.]1 [A]2 [E]1 [F]1 [G]2 [H]2
[I]2 [K]2 [N]4 [O]3 [S]2 [T]2

OUR REDEEMER LIVES!
[!]1 [D]1 [E]5 [I]1 [L]1
[M]1 [O]1 [R]3 [S]1 [U]1 [V]1

WHEN HE WAS ON
THE CROSS, YOU
WERE ON HIS MIND.
— ANONYMOUS
[,]1 [.]1 [A]1 [C]1 [D]1 [E]5 [H]4 [I]2
[M]1 [N]4 [O]4 [R]2 [S]4 [T]1 [U]1 [W]3 [Y]1
[A]1 [M]1 [N]2 [O]2 [S]1 [U]1 [Y]1 [—]1

Earth Day

THE BEST WAY TO
SAVE THE EARTH
IS TO SAVE ITS
INHABITANTS.

[.]1 [A]6 [B]2 [E]6 [H]4 [I]4 [N]2
[O]2 [R]1 [S]6 [T]9 [V]2 [W]1 [Y]1

LET THE
EARTH REJOICE!

[!]1 [A]1 [C]1 [E]5 [H]2
[I]1 [J]1 [L]1 [O]1 [R]2 [T]3

Mother's Day

THE MOTHER'S HEART IS
THE CHILD'S SCHOOLROOM.
— HENRY WARD BEECHER

[']2 [.]1 [A]1 [C]2 [D]1 [E]4 [H]6
[I]2 [L]2 [M]2 [O]5 [R]3 [S]4 [T]4
[A]1 [B]1 [C]1 [D]1 [E]4 [H]2 [N]1 [R]3 [W]1 [Y]1 [—]1

HI, MOMS!

[!]1 [,]1 [H]1
[I]1 [M]2 [O]1 [S]1

THE MOST IMPORTANT THING
A FATHER CAN DO FOR HIS
CHILDREN IS LOVE THEIR
MOTHER. — T. M. HERBURGH

[.]1 [A]4 [C]2 [D]2 [E]6 [F]2 [G]1 [H]7 [I]6
[L]2 [M]3 [N]4 [O]6 [P]1 [R]6 [S]3 [T]8 [V]1
[.]2 [B]1 [E]1 [G]1 [H]2 [M]1 [R]2 [T]1 [U]1 [—]1

MEN ARE WHAT THEIR
MOTHERS MADE THEM.
— EMERSON

    [.]1 [A]3 [D]1 [E]6 [H]4 [I]1
    [M]4 [N]1 [O]1 [R]3 [S]1 [T]4 [W]1
    [E]2 [M]1 [N]1 [O]1 [R]1 [S]1 [—]1

HAVE YOU HUGGED
YOUR MOTHER TODAY?

    [?]1 [A]2 [D]2 [E]3 [G]2 [H]3
    [M]1 [O]4 [R]2 [T]2 [U]3 [V]1 [Y]3

GOD COULDN'T BE
EVERYWHERE, SO HE
MADE MOTHERS.
— JEWISH PROVERB

    [']1 [,]1 [.]1 [A]1 [B]1 [C]1 [D]3 [E]8 [G]1 [H]3
    [L]1 [M]2 [N]1 [O]4 [R]3 [S]2 [T]2 [U]1 [V]1 [W]1 [Y]1
    [B]1 [E]2 [H]1 [I]1 [J]1 [O]1 [P]1 [R]2 [S]1 [V]1 [W]1 [—]1

Summer

GOD BLESS
OUR TEACHERS.
GOD HELP
OUR PARENTS.

    [.]2 [A]2 [B]1 [C]1 [D]2 [E]5 [G]2 [H]2
    [L]2 [N]1 [O]4 [P]2 [R]4 [S]4 [T]2 [U]2

**FIND SOMEONE
TO SHARE A SHAKE
AND YOUR FAITH WITH.**
[.]1 [A]5 [D]2 [E]4 [F]2 [H]4 [I]3 [K]1
[M]1 [N]3 [O]4 [R]2 [S]3 [T]3 [U]1 [W]1 [Y]1

Fourth of July

GOD BLESS AMERICA!
[!]1 [A]2 [B]1 [C]1 [D]1 [E]2
[G]1 [I]1 [L]1 [M]1 [O]1 [R]1 [S]2

**ARE YOU EXERCISING
YOUR FREEDOM
TO WORSHIP?**
[?]1 [A]1 [C]1 [D]1 [E]5 [F]1 [G]1 [H]1 [I]3 [M]1
[N]1 [O]5 [P]1 [R]5 [S]2 [T]1 [U]2 [W]1 [X]1 [Y]2

**GOD HAS GIVEN YOU
YOUR COUNTRY
AS A CRADLE.
— GIUSEPPE MAZZINI**
[.]1 [A]4 [C]2 [D]2 [E]2 [G]2 [H]1 [I]1
[L]1 [N]2 [O]4 [R]3 [S]2 [T]1 [U]3 [V]1 [Y]3
[A]1 [E]2 [G]1 [I]3 [M]1 [N]1 [P]2 [S]1 [U]1 [Z]2 [—]1

**O MY BROTHERS!
LOVE YOUR COUNTRY.
— GIUSEPPE MAZZINI**
[!]1 [.]1 [B]1 [C]1 [E]2 [H]1 [L]1 [M]1
[N]1 [O]5 [R]4 [S]1 [T]2 [U]2 [V]1 [Y]3
[A]1 [E]2 [G]1 [I]3 [M]1 [N]1 [P]2 [S]1 [U]1 [Z]2 [—]1

163

WHERE LIBERTY DWELLS
THERE IS OUR COUNTRY.
— REVISED JAMES OTIS
[.]1 [B]1 [C]1 [D]1 [E]6 [H]2 [I]2 [L]3
[N]1 [O]2 [R]5 [S]2 [T]3 [U]2 [W]2 [Y]2
[A]1 [D]1 [E]3 [I]2 [J]1 [M]1 [O]1 [R]1 [S]3 [T]1 [V]1 [—]1

THIS LAND WAS MADE
FOR YOU AND ME.
— GOD
[—]1 [.]1 [A]4 [D]4 [E]2 [F]1 [G]1 [H]1 [I]1
[L]1 [M]2 [N]2 [O]3 [R]1 [S]2 [T]1 [U]1 [W]1 [Y]1

NEXT TO LOVE OF GOD,
LOVE OF COUNTRY IS
THE BEST PREVENTIVE
OF CRIME. — GEORGE BORROW
[,]1 [.]1 [B]1 [C]2 [D]1 [E]9 [F]3 [G]1 [H]1 [I]3 [L]2
[M]1 [N]3 [O]8 [P]1 [R]3 [S]2 [T]6 [U]1 [V]4 [X]1 [Y]1
[B]1 [E]2 [G]2 [O]3 [R]3 [W]1 [—]1

Father's Day

FATHER'S DAY:
A TRIBUTE TO
GOOD MEN GONE DAD.
[']1 [.]1 [:]1 [A]4 [B]1 [D]4 [E]4 [F]1 [G]2
[H]1 [I]1 [M]1 [N]2 [O]4 [R]2 [S]1 [T]4 [U]1 [Y]1

TO REALLY AMOUNT
TO SOMETHING,
KIDS NEED
FATHER FIGURES.

[,]1 [.]1 [A]3 [D]2 [E]6 [F]2 [G]2 [H]2 [I]3
[K]1 [L]2 [M]2 [N]3 [O]4 [R]3 [S]3 [T]5 [U]2 [Y]1

IT IS A WISE FATHER
THAT KNOWS
HIS OWN CHILD.
— SHAKESPEARE

[.]1 [A]3 [C]1 [D]1 [E]2 [F]1 [H]4 [I]5
[K]1 [L]1 [N]2 [O]2 [R]1 [S]4 [T]4 [W]3
[A]2 [E]3 [H]1 [K]1 [P]1 [R]1 [S]2 [—]1

ONE FATHER IS
WORTH MORE THAN
A HUNDRED TEACHERS.

[.]1 [A]4 [C]1 [D]2 [E]6 [F]1 [H]5 [I]1
[M]1 [N]3 [O]3 [R]5 [S]2 [T]4 [U]1 [W]1

BLESSED IS THE MAN
WHO HEARS A SMALL
VOICE CALL HIM FATHER!
— REVISED LYDIA M. CHILD

[!]1 [A]6 [B]1 [C]2 [D]1 [E]6 [F]1 [H]5 [I]3
[L]5 [M]3 [N]1 [O]2 [R]2 [S]5 [T]2 [V]1 [W]1
[.]1 [A]1 [C]1 [D]3 [E]2 [H]1 [I]3 [L]2 [M]1 [R]1 [S]1 [V]1 [Y]1 [—]1

IT'S FATHER TIME!

[!]1 [']1 [A]1 [E]2 [F]1 [H]1
[I]2 [M]1 [R]1 [S]1 [T]3

165

**THIS IS YOUR
CHANCE TO TURN
BACK THE CLOCK.**
> [.]1 [A]2 [B]1 [C]5 [E]2 [H]3 [I]2 [K]2
> [L]1 [N]2 [O]3 [R]2 [S]2 [T]4 [U]2 [Y]1

**TIMES CHANGE,
BUT GOD REMAINS
THE SAME.**
> [,]1 [.]1 [A]3 [B]1 [C]1 [D]1 [E]5 [G]2
> [H]2 [I]2 [M]3 [N]2 [O]1 [R]1 [S]3 [T]3 [U]1

**TIMES CHANGE,
AND SO SHOULD WE.**
> [,]1 [.]1 [A]2 [C]1 [D]2 [E]3 [G]1 [H]2
> [I]1 [L]1 [M]1 [N]2 [O]2 [S]3 [T]1 [U]1 [W]1

**SPRING FORWARD,
FALL BACK ON GOD.**
> [,]1 [.]1 [A]3 [B]1 [C]1 [D]2 [F]2 [G]2
> [I]1 [K]1 [L]2 [N]2 [O]3 [P]1 [R]3 [S]1 [W]1

**SPRING FORWARD
WITH GOD
THIS SUNDAY.**
> [.]1 [A]2 [D]3 [F]1 [G]2 [H]2 [I]3 [N]2
> [O]2 [P]1 [R]3 [S]3 [T]2 [U]1 [W]2 [Y]1

FALL BACK
INTO THE
CHURCH HABIT
THIS SUNDAY.
[.]1 [A]4 [B]2 [C]3 [D]1 [E]1 [F]1 [H]5 [I]3
[K]1 [L]2 [N]2 [O]1 [R]1 [S]2 [T]4 [U]2 [Y]1

SPRING FORWARD
THIS SUNDAY
WITH RENEWED JOY.
[.]1 [A]2 [D]3 [E]3 [F]1 [G]1 [H]2 [I]3 [J]1
[N]3 [O]2 [P]1 [R]4 [S]3 [T]2 [U]1 [W]3 [Y]2

Back to School

TO ALL
OUR TEACHERS:
GODSPEED!
[!]1 [:]1 [A]2 [C]1 [D]2 [E]4 [G]1
[H]1 [L]2 [O]3 [P]1 [R]2 [S]2 [T]2 [U]1

THOSE WHO CAN, DO.
THOSE WHO BELIEVE
YOU CAN TOO, TEACH.
[,]2 [.]2 [A]3 [B]1 [C]3 [D]1 [E]6 [H]5 [I]1
[L]1 [N]2 [O]8 [S]2 [T]4 [U]1 [V]1 [W]2 [Y]1

THE BIBLE'S YOUR TEXT.
TEMPTATION'S THE TEST.
LIFE'S THE LAB.
[']3 [.]3 [A]2 [B]3 [E]8 [F]1 [H]3 [I]3 [L]3
[M]1 [N]1 [O]2 [P]1 [R]1 [S]4 [T]10 [U]1 [X]1 [Y]1

IF YOU CAN COUNT
YOUR BLESSINGS,
THANK A TEACHER.
[,]1 [.]1 [A]4 [B]1 [C]3 [E]3 [F]1 [G]1 [H]2
[I]2 [K]1 [L]1 [N]4 [O]3 [R]2 [S]3 [T]3 [U]3 [Y]2

EDUCATION IS WHAT
SURVIVES WHEN WHAT
WAS LEARNED IS
FORGOTTEN. — B. F. SKINNER
[.]1 [A]5 [C]1 [D]2 [E]6 [F]1 [G]1 [H]3 [I]4
[L]1 [N]4 [O]3 [R]3 [S]5 [T]5 [U]2 [V]2 [W]4
[.]2 [B]1 [E]1 [F]1 [I]1 [K]1 [N]2 [R]1 [S]1 [—]1

Fall

OUR FALL FESTIVAL
IS A BLESSING
IN DISGUISE.
[.]1 [A]3 [B]1 [D]1 [E]3 [F]2 [G]2 [I]6
[L]4 [N]2 [O]1 [R]1 [S]6 [T]1 [U]2 [V]1

SEASONS CHANGE.
GOD DOESN'T.
[']1 [.]2 [A]2 [C]1 [D]2 [E]3
[G]2 [H]1 [N]3 [O]3 [S]4 [T]1

Election Day

CHOOSE THIS
DAY WHOM
YOU WILL SERVE.
— JOSHUA 24:15
    [—]1 [.]1 [1]1 [2]1 [4]1 [5]1 [:]1 [A]2 [C]1 [D]1 [E]3 [H]4
    [I]2 [J]1 [L]2 [M]1 [O]5 [R]1 [S]4 [T]1 [U]2 [V]1 [W]2 [Y]2

CHOOSE THIS DAY
WHO WILL SERVE YOU.
— FOUNDING FATHERS
    [—]1 [.]1 [A]2 [C]1 [D]2 [E]4 [F]2 [G]1 [H]4 [I]3
    [L]2 [N]2 [O]5 [R]2 [S]4 [T]2 [U]2 [V]1 [W]2 [Y]2

IT TAKES BOTH A RIGHT
WING AND LEFT WING
FOR A BIRD TO FLY.
VOTE TODAY.
    [.]2 [A]5 [B]2 [D]3 [E]3 [F]3 [G]3 [H]2 [I]5
    [K]1 [L]2 [N]3 [O]5 [R]3 [S]1 [T]8 [V]1 [W]2 [Y]2

Thanksgiving

LET YOUR
PRAISES RING.
    [.]1 [A]1 [E]2 [G]1 [I]2 [L]1 [N]1
    [O]1 [P]1 [R]3 [S]2 [T]1 [U]1 [Y]1

**BE THANKFUL TODAY
AND AVOID
THE HOLIDAY RUSH.**
    [.]1 [A]5 [B]1 [D]4 [E]2 [F]1 [H]4 [I]2 [K]1
    [L]2 [N]2 [O]3 [R]1 [S]1 [T]3 [U]2 [V]1 [Y]2

**WE GATHER TOGETHER
TO ASK
THE LORD'S BLESSING.**
    [']1 [.]1 [A]2 [B]1 [D]1 [E]6 [G]3 [H]3
    [I]1 [K]1 [L]2 [N]1 [O]3 [R]3 [S]4 [T]5 [W]1

**SING PRAISES
TO HIS NAME;
HE FORGETS NOT
HIS OWN.**
    [.]1 [;]1 [A]2 [E]4 [F]1 [G]2 [H]3 [I]4
    [M]1 [N]4 [O]4 [P]1 [R]2 [S]6 [T]3 [W]1

Winter

**GOD GAVE US MEMORIES
THAT WE MIGHT HAVE
ROSES IN DECEMBER.
— SIR JAMES M. BARRIE**
    [.]1 [A]3 [B]1 [C]1 [D]2 [E]9 [G]3 [H]3 [I]3
    [M]4 [N]1 [O]3 [R]3 [S]4 [T]3 [U]1 [V]2 [W]1
    [.]1 [A]2 [B]1 [E]2 [I]2 [J]1 [M]2 [R]3 [S]2 [—]1

IF WINTER COMES,
CAN SPRING BE
FAR BEHIND?
— SHELLEY

[,]1 [?]1 [A]2 [B]2 [C]2 [D]1 [E]4 [F]2 [G]1
[H]1 [I]4 [M]1 [N]4 [O]1 [P]1 [R]3 [S]2 [T]1 [W]1
[E]2 [H]1 [L]2 [S]1 [Y]1 [—]1

IF DARK WINTER DAYS
ARE HERE, CAN
RESURRECTION SUNDAY
BE FAR BEHIND?

[,]1 [?]1 [A]6 [B]2 [C]2 [D]4 [E]8 [F]2 [H]2
[I]4 [K]1 [N]5 [O]1 [R]8 [S]3 [T]2 [U]2 [W]1 [Y]2

DURING THE
DEEPEST WINTER,
WE EACH KEEP
A PIECE OF SPRING.

[,]1 [.]1 [A]2 [C]2 [D]2 [E]11 [F]1 [G]2 [H]2
[I]4 [K]1 [N]3 [O]1 [P]4 [R]3 [S]2 [T]3 [U]1 [W]2

IT'S A GOOD TIME
TO THANK GOD
FOR WARM FRIENDS.

[']1 [.]1 [A]3 [D]3 [E]2 [F]2 [G]2 [H]1
[I]3 [K]1 [M]2 [N]2 [O]5 [R]3 [S]2 [T]4 [W]1

FOR UNTO US
IS THE
CHRIST CHILD GIVEN.
[.]1 [C]2 [D]1 [E]2 [F]1 [G]1 [H]3 [I]4
[L]1 [N]2 [O]2 [R]2 [S]3 [T]3 [U]2 [V]1

REMEMBER WHY
HE CAME?
[?]1 [A]1 [B]1 [C]1 [E]5
[H]2 [M]3 [R]2 [W]1 [Y]1

LET IT RING:
HE IS BORN!
[!]1 [:]1 [B]1 [E]2 [G]1 [H]1
[I]3 [L]1 [N]2 [O]1 [R]2 [S]1 [T]2

DO YOU HEAR
WHAT WE HEAR?
[?]1 [A]3 [D]1 [E]3 [H]3
[O]2 [R]2 [T]1 [U]1 [W]2 [Y]1

HAPPY HOLYDAYS!
[!]1 [A]2 [D]1 [H]2
[L]1 [O]1 [P]2 [S]1 [Y]3

CELEBRATE THE BIRTH
OF THE BOY
WHO WOULD BE KING.
[.]1 [A]1 [B]4 [C]1 [D]1 [E]6 [F]1 [G]1 [H]4
[I]2 [K]1 [L]2 [N]1 [O]4 [R]2 [T]4 [U]1 [W]2 [Y]1

HAIL THE BIRTHDAY
OF THE KING.
   [.]1 [A]2 [B]1 [D]1 [E]2 [F]1 [G]1 [H]4
   [I]3 [K]1 [L]1 [N]1 [O]1 [R]1 [T]3 [Y]1

ALL CREATION
REJOICES
AT HIS BIRTH.
   [.]1 [A]3 [B]1 [C]2 [E]3 [H]2 [I]4
   [J]1 [L]2 [N]1 [O]2 [R]3 [S]2 [T]3

CONGRATS TO THE FATHER
UPON THE BIRTH
OF THE SON.
   [.]1 [A]2 [B]1 [C]1 [E]4 [F]2 [G]1 [H]5
   [I]1 [N]3 [O]5 [P]1 [R]3 [S]2 [T]7 [U]1

BELLS ARE RINGING
AT HIS BIRTH.
LET'S ALL CHIME IN.
   [']1 [.]2 [A]3 [B]2 [C]1 [E]4 [G]2
   [H]3 [I]6 [L]5 [M]1 [N]3 [R]3 [S]3 [T]3

JOSEPH WAS THE
FIRST TO BE IN A
CHRISTMAS RUSH.
   [.]1 [A]3 [B]1 [C]1 [E]3 [F]1 [H]4 [I]3 [J]1
   [M]1 [N]1 [O]2 [P]1 [R]3 [S]6 [T]4 [U]1 [W]1

LET'S GIVE JESUS
A BIRTHDAY
WITH ALL
THE TRIMMINGS.

[']1 [.]1 [A]3 [B]1 [D]1 [E]4 [G]2 [H]3 [I]5 [J]1
[L]3 [M]2 [N]1 [R]2 [S]4 [T]5 [U]1 [V]1 [W]1 [Y]1

Under Construction

PARDON OUR DUST.
WE'RE JUST
FOLLOWING THE
CARPENTER'S ORDERS.

[']2 [.]2 [A]2 [C]1 [D]3 [E]6 [F]1 [G]1 [H]1 [I]1
[J]1 [L]2 [N]3 [O]5 [P]2 [R]7 [S]4 [T]4 [U]3 [W]2

WE'RE BIGGER.
COME HELP
MAKE US BETTER.

[']1 [.]2 [A]1 [B]2 [C]1 [E]8 [G]2 [H]1 [I]1
[K]1 [L]1 [M]2 [O]1 [P]1 [R]3 [S]1 [T]2 [U]1 [W]1

WE'RE BUSTIN'
AT THE SEAMS
WITH FUN.

[']2 [.]1 [A]2 [B]1 [E]4 [F]1 [H]2
[I]2 [M]1 [N]2 [R]1 [S]3 [T]4 [U]2 [W]2

WE'RE EXPECTING,
SO WE DECIDED
TO ADD ON.

[']1 [,]1 [.]1 [A]1 [C]2 [D]5 [E]7 [G]1
[I]2 [N]2 [O]3 [P]1 [R]1 [S]1 [T]2 [W]2 [X]1

174

LITTLE BY LITTLE
WE'RE GETTING
BIGGER AND BETTER.
['1 [.]1 [A]1 [B]3 [D]1 [E]8 [G]4
[I]4 [L]4 [N]2 [R]3 [T]8 [W]1 [Y]1

(building a gym or family life center)

WE'RE ADDING
ON A PLAYROOM.
['1 [.]1 [A]3 [D]2 [E]2 [G]1 [I]1
[L]1 [M]1 [N]2 [O]3 [P]1 [R]2 [W]1 [Y]1

(building a family life center)

PARDON OUR
CONSTRUCTION.
WE'RE IN THE
FAMILY WAY.
['1 [.]2 [A]3 [C]2 [D]1 [E]3 [F]1 [H]1 [I]3 [L]1
[M]1 [N]4 [O]4 [P]1 [R]4 [S]1 [T]3 [U]2 [W]2 [Y]2

To Forgive Is Divine

On walking softly and carrying an olive branch

FEED A GRUDGE,
STARVE A FRIENDSHIP.
[,]1 [.]1 [A]3 [D]3 [E]5 [F]2 [G]2 [H]1
[I]2 [N]1 [P]1 [R]3 [S]2 [T]1 [U]1 [V]1

BETTER TO FORGIVE
AND FORGET THAN
RESENT AND REMEMBER.
— ANONYMOUS
[.]1 [A]3 [B]2 [D]2 [E]9 [F]2 [G]2 [H]1
[I]1 [M]2 [N]4 [O]3 [R]6 [S]1 [T]6 [V]1
[A]1 [M]1 [N]2 [O]2 [S]1 [U]1 [Y]1 [—]1

IT IS EASIER TO
FORGIVE AN ENEMY
THAN A FRIEND.
— DOROTHEE DELUZY
[.]1 [A]4 [D]1 [E]6 [F]2 [G]1 [H]1 [I]5
[M]1 [N]4 [O]2 [R]3 [S]2 [T]3 [V]1 [Y]1
[D]2 [E]3 [H]1 [L]1 [O]2 [R]1 [T]1 [U]1 [Y]1 [Z]1 [—]1

FORGIVENESS IS
THE FINAL FORM
OF LOVE.
— REINHOLD NIEBUHR
[.]1 [A]1 [E]4 [F]4 [G]1 [H]1 [I]3
[L]2 [M]1 [N]2 [O]4 [R]2 [S]3 [T]1 [V]2
[B]1 [D]1 [E]2 [H]2 [I]2 [L]1 [N]2 [O]1 [R]2 [U]1 [—]1

**FORGIVE ALL WHO HAVE
OFFENDED YOU — NOT FOR
THEM, BUT FOR YOURSELF.
— HARRIET NELSON**

[,]1 [—]1 [.]1 [A]2 [B]1 [D]2 [E]6 [F]6 [G]1 [H]3 [I]1
[L]3 [M]1 [N]2 [O]8 [R]4 [S]1 [T]3 [U]3 [V]2 [W]1 [Y]2
[A]1 [E]2 [H]1 [I]1 [L]1 [N]2 [O]1 [R]2 [S]1 [T]1 [—]1

**GRACE IS
FOR GIVING.
FORGIVING IS
FORGETTING.**

[.]2 [A]1 [C]1 [E]2 [F]3 [G]7
[I]7 [N]3 [O]3 [R]4 [S]2 [T]2 [V]2

**WHEN WE'RE ALL
STEAMED UP, IT
USUALLY BOILS
DOWN TO NOTHING.**

[']1 [,]1 [.]1 [A]3 [B]1 [D]2 [E]5 [G]1 [H]2 [I]3
[L]5 [M]1 [N]4 [O]4 [P]1 [R]1 [S]3 [T]4 [U]3 [W]3 [Y]1

**WE WON'T BE SO
AT ODDS WHEN
WE FORGET ABOUT
GETTING EVEN.**

[']1 [.]1 [A]2 [B]2 [D]2 [E]8 [F]1 [G]3 [H]1
[I]1 [N]4 [O]5 [R]1 [S]2 [T]6 [U]1 [V]1 [W]4

Two-Edged Swords
For Two-Sided Marquees

When a single subject deserves a double whammy

DO THE RIGHT THING.
[.]1 [D]1 [E]1 [G]2 [H]3
[I]2 [N]1 [O]1 [R]1 [T]3

IT'S THE RIGHT THING TO DO.
[']1 [.]1 [D]1 [E]1 [G]2 [H]3
[I]3 [N]1 [O]2 [R]1 [S]1 [T]5

* * *

FAITH IS TO BELIEVE
WHAT WE DO NOT SEE.
— ST. AUGUSTINE
[.]1 [A]2 [B]1 [D]1 [E]6 [F]1 [H]2
[I]3 [L]1 [N]1 [O]3 [S]2 [T]4 [V]1 [W]2
[.]1 [A]1 [E]1 [G]1 [I]1 [N]1 [S]2 [T]2 [U]2 [—]1

THE REWARD OF FAITH
IS TO SEE
WHAT WE BELIEVE.
— ST. AUGUSTINE
[.]1 [A]3 [B]1 [D]1 [E]8 [F]2 [H]3
[I]3 [L]1 [O]2 [R]2 [S]2 [T]4 [V]1 [W]3
[.]1 [A]1 [E]1 [G]1 [I]1 [N]1 [S]2 [T]2 [U]2 [—]1

* * *

THE BATHROOM'S DOWN
THE HALL ON THE LEFT.
[']1 [.]1 [A]2 [B]1 [D]1 [E]4 [F]1 [H]5
[L]3 [M]1 [N]2 [O]4 [R]1 [S]1 [T]5 [W]1

JUST WANTED TO MAKE
YOU FEEL AT HOME.
[.]1 [A]3 [D]1 [E]5 [F]1 [H]1 [J]1 [K]1
[L]1 [M]2 [N]1 [O]3 [S]1 [T]4 [U]2 [W]1 [Y]1

* * *

DON'T WATCH
THIS SPACE.
[']1 [.]1 [A]2 [C]2 [D]1 [E]1 [H]2
[I]1 [N]1 [O]1 [P]1 [S]2 [T]3 [W]1

KEEP YOUR EYES
ON JESUS.
[.]1 [E]5 [J]1 [K]1 [N]1 [O]2
[P]1 [R]1 [S]3 [U]2 [Y]2
[A]1 [M]1 [N]2 [O]2 [S]1 [U]1 [Y]1 [—]1

* * *

JESUS IS
COMING.
[.]1 [C]1 [E]1 [G]1 [I]2
[J]1 [M]1 [N]1 [O]1 [S]3 [U]1

GET RIGHT
OR GET LEFT.
— ANONYMOUS
[.]1 [E]3 [F]1 [G]3 [H]1
[I]1 [L]1 [O]1 [R]2 [T]4
[A]1 [M]1 [N]2 [O]2 [S]1 [U]1 [Y]1 [—]1

* * *

**MY CHILDREN,
DON'T TAKE MY
DISCIPLINE LIGHTLY.**

— HEBREWS 12:5

[']1 [,]1 [—]1 [.]1 [1]1 [2]1 [5]1 [:]1 [A]1 [B]1
[C]2 [D]3 [E]5 [G]1 [H]3 [I]5 [K]1 [L]4 [M]2
[N]3 [O]1 [P]1 [R]2 [S]2 [T]3 [W]1 [Y]3

**THOSE WHOM I LOVE,
I DISCIPLINE.**

— HEBREWS 12:6

[,]1 [—]1 [.]1 [1]1 [2]1 [6]1 [:]1 [B]1 [C]1 [D]1 [E]5
[H]3 [I]5 [L]2 [M]1 [N]1 [O]3 [P]1 [R]1 [S]3 [T]1 [V]1 [W]2

*   *   *

**HATE CANNOT DRIVE OUT
HATE; ONLY LOVE
CAN DO THAT.**

— M. L. KING, JR.

[.]1 [;]1 [A]5 [C]2 [D]2 [E]4 [H]3 [I]1
[L]2 [N]4 [O]5 [R]1 [T]6 [U]1 [V]2 [Y]1
[,]1 [.]3 [G]1 [I]1 [J]1 [K]1 [L]1 [M]1 [N]1 [R]1 [—]1

**DARKNESS CANNOT DRIVE
OUT DARKNESS; ONLY
LIGHT CAN DO THAT.**

— M. L. KING, JR.

[.]1 [;]1 [A]5 [C]2 [D]4 [E]3 [G]1 [H]2 [I]2
[K]2 [L]2 [N]6 [O]4 [R]3 [S]4 [T]5 [U]1 [V]1 [Y]1
[,]1 [.]3 [G]1 [I]1 [J]1 [K]1 [L]1 [M]1 [N]1 [R]1 [—]1

*   *   *

THE BIBLE IS
A DIVINE HELP BOOK.
[.]1 [A]1 [B]3 [D]1 [E]4 [H]2 [I]4
[K]1 [L]2 [N]1 [O]2 [P]1 [S]1 [T]1 [V]1

THE BIBLE ISN'T
A SELF-HELP BOOK.
[']1 [-]1 [.]1 [A]1 [B]3 [E]4 [F]1 [H]2
[I]2 [K]1 [L]3 [N]1 [O]2 [P]1 [S]2 [T]2

*   *   *

THE SIZE
OF YOUR BRAIN
MATTERS LITTLE.
[.]1 [A]2 [B]1 [E]4 [F]1 [H]1 [I]3 [L]2
[M]1 [N]1 [O]2 [R]3 [S]2 [T]5 [U]1 [Y]1 [Z]1

THE SIZE
OF YOUR HEART
MATTERS MUCH.
[.]1 [A]2 [C]1 [E]4 [F]1 [H]3 [I]1
[M]2 [O]2 [R]3 [S]2 [T]4 [U]2 [Y]1 [Z]1

*   *   *

COME TO ME
AS LITTLE CHILDREN.
— MATTHEW 18:3
[—]1 [.]1 [1]1 [3]1 [8]1 [:]1 [A]2 [C]2 [D]1 [E]5
[H]2 [I]2 [L]3 [M]3 [N]1 [O]2 [R]1 [S]1 [T]5 [W]1

FAITH IS KID STUFF.
[.]1 [A]1 [D]1 [F]3 [H]1
[I]3 [K]1 [S]2 [T]2 [U]1

*   *   *

JOHN DOE, MUSIC MINISTER
MARY SMITH, PASTOR.
[,]2 [.]1 [A]2 [C]1 [D]1 [E]2 [H]1 [I]4 [J]1
[M]4 [N]2 [O]3 [P]1 [R]3 [S]4 [T]3 [U]1 [Y]1

(*Substitute your own music minister's and pastor's names in place of John Doe and Mary Smith. The letter count is for the words* MUSIC MINISTER *and* PASTOR *only.*)

JESUS CHRIST, CEO.
[,]1 [.]1 [C]2 [E]2 [H]1 [I]1
[J]1 [O]1 [R]1 [S]3 [T]1 [U]1

* * *

CREATE IN ME A
CLEAN HEART, O GOD.
— PROVERBS 51:10
[,]1 [—]1 [.]1 [0]1 [1]2 [5]1 [:]1 [A]4 [B]1 [C]2 [D]1
[E]6 [G]1 [H]1 [I]1 [L]1 [M]1 [N]2 [O]3 [P]1 [R]4 [S]1 [T]2 [V]1

RENEW A
RIGHT SPIRIT
WITHIN ME.
— PROVERBS 51:10
[—]1 [.]1 [0]1 [1]2 [5]1 [:]1 [A]1 [B]1 [E]4 [G]1
[H]2 [I]5 [M]1 [N]2 [O]1 [P]2 [R]5 [S]2 [T]3 [V]1 [W]2

* * *

GOD'S GRACE:
USE IT
RESPONSIBLY.
    [']1 [.]1 [:]1 [A]1 [B]1 [C]1 [D]1 [E]3 [G]2
    [I]2 [L]1 [N]1 [O]2 [P]1 [R]2 [S]4 [T]1 [U]1 [Y]1

GOD'S LOVE:
USE IT
UNCONDITIONALLY.
    [']1 [.]1 [:]1 [A]1 [C]1 [D]2 [E]2 [G]1
    [I]3 [L]3 [N]3 [O]4 [S]2 [T]2 [U]2 [V]1 [Y]1

* * *

TOUCH BASE
WITH GOD
BEFORE YOU
STRIKE OUT.
    [.]1 [A]1 [B]2 [C]1 [D]1 [Ė]4 [F]1 [G]1
    [H]2 [I]2 [K]1 [O]5 [R]2 [S]2 [T]4 [U]3 [W]1 [Y]1

IF YOU'RE SLIDING,
TOUCH BASE
WITH THE SAVIOR.
    [']1 [,]1 [.]1 [A]2 [B]1 [C]1 [D]1 [E]3 [F]1 [G]1 [H]3
    [I]5 [L]1 [N]1 [O]3 [R]2 [S]3 [T]3 [U]2 [V]1 [W]1 [Y]1

* * *

NO SHIRT
NO SHOES
NO PROBLEM
    [B]1 [E]2 [H]2 [I]1 [L]1 [M]1
    [N]3 [O]5 [P]1 [R]2 [S]3 [T]1

SUNDAY BEST
NOT REQUIRED.
    [.]1 [A]1 [B]1 [D]2 [E]3 [I]1 [N]2
    [O]1 [Q]1 [R]2 [S]2 [T]2 [U]2 [Y]1

* * *

CHRISTIANITY ISN'T
A COVERT OPERATION.
    [']1 [.]1 [A]3 [C]2 [E]2 [H]1 [I]5
    [N]3 [O]3 [P]1 [R]3 [S]2 [T]5 [V]1 [Y]1

CHRISTIANITY IS A
CONVERT OPERATION.
    [.]1 [A]3 [C]2 [E]2 [H]1 [I]5 [N]3
    [O]3 [P]1 [R]3 [S]2 [T]4 [V]1 [Y]1

* * *

THE RELIGION OF JESUS
BEGINS WITH
THE VERB "FOLLOW..."
— ANONYMOUS
["]1 ["]1 [.]3 [B]2 [E]6 [F]2 [G]2 [H]3 [I]4 [J]1
[L]3 [N]2 [O]4 [R]2 [S]3 [T]3 [U]1 [V]1 [W]2
[A]1 [M]1 [N]2 [O]2 [S]1 [U]1 [Y]1 [—]1

THE RELIGION OF JESUS
ENDS WITH
THE WORD "GO."
— ANONYMOUS
["]1 ["]1 [.]1 [D]2 [E]5 [F]1 [G]2 [H]3 [I]3
[J]1 [L]1 [N]2 [O]4 [R]2 [S]3 [T]3 [U]1 [W]2
[A]1 [M]1 [N]2 [O]2 [S]1 [U]1 [Y]1 [—]1

* * *

NOW OFFERING
CHRISTIAN LIVING
TO GO.
[.]1 [A]1 [C]1 [E]1 [F]2 [G]3 [H]1
[I]5 [L]1 [N]4 [O]4 [R]2 [S]1 [T]2 [V]1 [W]1

TODAY'S SPECIAL:
A VALUES PACK.
[']1 [.] [:]1 [A]5 [C]2 [D]1 [E]2 [I]1 [K]1
[L]2 [O]1 [P]2 [S]3 [T]1 [U]1 [V]1 [Y]1

* * *

CATCH SOME G'S:
GENTLENESS,
GOODNESS,
GRACE
    [']1 [,]2 [:]1 [A]2 [C]3 [D]1 [E]6 [G]4
    [H]1 [L]1 [M]1 [N]3 [O]3 [R]1 [S]6 [T]2

CATCH SOME P'S:
PURITY,
PATIENCE,
PEACE
    [']1 [,]2 [:]1 [A]3 [C]4 [E]5 [H]1 [I]2
    [M]1 [N]1 [O]1 [P]4 [R]1 [S]2 [T]3 [U]1 [Y]1

*   *   *

CONVENTIONAL WISDOM
SAYS SOME PEOPLE
ARE HOPELESS.
    [.]1 [A]3 [C]1 [D]1 [E]7 [H]1 [I]2 [L]3
    [M]2 [N]3 [O]6 [P]3 [R]1 [S]6 [T]1 [V]1 [W]1 [Y]1

THANK HEAVEN
GOD'S WISDOM
ISN'T CONVENTIONAL.
    [']2 [.]1 [A]3 [C]1 [D]2 [E]3 [G]1 [H]2 [I]3
    [K]1 [L]1 [M]1 [N]6 [O]4 [S]3 [T]3 [V]2 [W]1

*   *   *

BEHIND EVERY
SUCCESSFUL CHRISTIAN
THERE'S TESTING.

[']1 [.]1 [A]1 [B]1 [C]3 [D]1 [E]7 [F]1 [G]1
[H]3 [I]4 [L]1 [N]3 [R]3 [S]6 [T]4 [U]2 [V]1 [Y]1

AHEAD OF EVERY
SUCCESSFUL CHRISTIAN
THERE'S A REWARD.

[']1 [.]1 [A]5 [C]3 [D]2 [E]7 [F]2 [H]3 [I]2
[L]1 [N]1 [O]1 [R]5 [S]5 [T]2 [U]2 [V]1 [W]1 [Y]1

*   *   *

WHAT DOES THE LORD
REQUIRE OF YOU?

[?]1 [A]1 [D]2 [E]4 [F]1 [H]2 [I]1
[L]1 [O]4 [Q]1 [R]3 [S]1 [T]2 [U]2 [W]1 [Y]1

ACT JUSTLY,
LOVE MERCY,
WALK HUMBLY
WITH YOUR GOD.

[,]2 [.]1 [A]2 [B]1 [C]2 [D]1 [E]2 [G]1 [H]2 [I]1 [J]1
[K]1 [L]4 [M]2 [O]3 [R]2 [S]1 [T]3 [U]3 [V]1 [W]2 [Y]4

*   *   *

188

DID YOU
BRUSH YOUR TEETH?
[?]1 [B]1 [D]2 [E]2 [H]2 [I]1
[O]2 [R]2 [S]1 [T]2 [U]3 [Y]2

JUST WANTED YOU
TO KNOW WE CONSIDER
YOU FAMILY.
[.]1 [A]2 [C]1 [D]2 [E]3 [F]1 [I]2 [J]1 [K]1
[L]1 [M]1 [N]3 [O]5 [R]1 [S]2 [T]3 [U]3 [W]3 [Y]3

*   *   *

A MAN OF WORDS AND
NOT OF DEEDS IS LIKE
A GARDEN FULL OF
WEEDS. — ANONYMOUS
[.]1 [A]5 [D]6 [E]6 [F]4 [G]1 [I]2 [K]1
[L]3 [M]1 [N]4 [O]5 [R]2 [S]4 [T]1 [U]1 [W]2
[A]1 [M]1 [N]2 [O]2 [S]1 [U]1 [Y]1 [—]1

A GOOD GARDEN
MAY HAVE SOME WEEDS.
— THOMAS FULLER
[.]1 [A]4 [D]3 [E]5 [G]2 [H]1 [M]2
[N]1 [O]3 [R]1 [S]2 [V]1 [W]1 [Y]1
[A]1 [E]1 [F]1 [H]1 [L]2 [M]1 [O]1 [R]1 [S]1 [T]1 [U]1 [—]1

*   *   *

**JESUS WENT ABOUT
DOING GOOD.**
[.]1 [A]1 [B]1 [D]2 [E]2 [G]2 [I]1
[J]1 [N]2 [O]4 [S]2 [T]2 [U]2 [W]1

**DO GOOD WITH
WHAT YOU HAVE
OR IT WILL DO
YOU NO GOOD.**
(*Wings of Silver*)
[.]1 [A]2 [D]4 [E]1 [G]2 [H]3 [I]3 [L]2
[N]1 [O]10 [R]1 [T]3 [U]2 [V]1 [W]3 [Y]2

Unconventional Wisdoms

Words to those who would be wise

**HOW DOES IT
ALL TURN OUT?
READ THE BOOK.**
 [.]1 [?]1 [A]2 [B]1 [D]2 [E]3 [H]2 [I]1
 [K]1 [L]2 [N]1 [O]5 [R]2 [S]1 [T]4 [U]2 [W]1

**SO TEACH US TO NUMBER
OUR DAYS, THAT WE MAY
APPLY OUR HEARTS UNTO
WISDOM. — PSALM 90:12**
 [,]1 [—]1 [.]1 [0]1 [1]1 [2]1 [9]1 [:]1 [A]7 [B]1 [C]1 [D]2 [E]4
 [H]3 [I]1 [L]2 [M]4 [N]2 [O]6 [P]3 [R]4 [S]6 [T]6 [U]5 [W]2 [Y]3

**TIME IS THE COIN OF
YOUR LIFE. DON'T LET
ANYONE SPEND IT FOR
YOU. — REVISED SANDBURG**
 [']1 [.]2 [A]1 [C]1 [D]2 [E]6 [F]3 [H]1 [I]5
 [L]2 [M]1 [N]5 [O]7 [P]1 [R]2 [S]2 [T]5 [U]2 [Y]3
 [A]1 [B]1 [D]2 [E]2 [G]1 [I]1 [N]1 [R]2 [S]2 [U]1 [V]1 [—]1

**THE ANSWERS
ARE AT THE BACK,
FRONT, AND MIDDLE
OF THE BOOK.**
 [,]2 [.]1 [A]5 [B]2 [C]1 [D]3 [E]6 [F]2 [H]3
 [I]1 [K]2 [L]1 [M]1 [N]3 [O]4 [R]3 [S]2 [T]5 [W]1

**EVEN A FOOL, WHEN
HE HOLDETH HIS PEACE,
IS COUNTED WISE.**
— **PROVERBS 17:27-28**

[,]2 [-]1 [—]1 [.]1 [1]1 [2]2 [7]2 [8]1 [:]1 [A]2
[B]1 [C]2 [D]2 [E]10 [F]1 [H]5 [I]3 [L]2 [N]3
[O]5 [P]2 [R]2 [S]4 [T]2 [U]1 [V]2 [W]2

**SOMETIMES YOU HAVE
TO ROCK THE BOAT
TO STILL THE STORM.**

[.]1 [A]2 [B]1 [C]1 [E]5 [H]3 [I]2 [K]1
[L]2 [M]3 [O]7 [R]2 [S]4 [T]8 [U]1 [V]1 [Y]1

**NOT EVERYTHING'S
A TRICK
OF THE DEVIL.**

[']1 [.]1 [A]1 [C]1 [D]1 [E]4 [F]1 [G]1 [H]2
[I]3 [K]1 [L]1 [N]2 [O]2 [R]2 [S]1 [T]4 [V]2 [Y]1

**FOR THE WISDOM OF
THIS WORLD IS
FOOLISHNESS WITH GOD.**
— **1 CORINTHIANS 3:19**

[—]1 [.]1 [1]2 [3]1 [9]1 [:]1 [A]1 [C]1 [D]3 [E]2 [F]3
[G]1 [H]5 [I]7 [L]2 [M]1 [N]3 [O]8 [R]3 [S]7 [T]4 [W]3

**MOSES DIDN'T BEAT
AROUND THE BUSH.**

[']1 [.]1 [A]2 [B]2 [D]3 [E]3 [H]2
[I]1 [M]1 [N]2 [O]2 [R]1 [S]3 [T]3 [U]2

**IF WE FAIL LIFE'S
TESTS, MAYBE IT'S
BECAUSE WE NEVER
CRACKED THE BOOK.**
['] 2 [,]1 [.]1 [A]4 [B]3 [C]3 [D]1 [E]11 [F]3 [H]1 [I]4
[K]2 [L]2 [M]1 [N]1 [O]2 [R]2 [S]5 [T]4 [U]1 [V]1 [W]2 [Y]1

**LESS IS MORE.
GOD IS IN THE DETAILS.
— LUDWIG MIES VAN DER ROHE**
[.]2 [A]1 [D]2 [E]4 [G]1 [H]1 [I]4
[L]2 [M]1 [N]1 [O]2 [R]1 [S]5 [T]2
[A]1 [D]2 [E]3 [G]1 [H]1 [I]2 [L]1 [M]1
[N]1 [O]1 [R]2 [S]1 [U]1 [V]1 [W]1 [—]1

**DON'T RUN TOO FAR.
YOU'LL HAVE TO RETURN
THE SAME DISTANCE.**
['] 2 [.]2 [A]4 [C]1 [D]2 [E]5 [F]1 [H]2 [I]1
[L]2 [M]1 [N]4 [O]5 [R]4 [S]2 [T]6 [U]3 [V]1 [Y]1

**IN CASE OF DOUBT,
IT IS BEST TO LEAN
TO THE SIDE OF MERCY.
— LEGAL PROVERB**
[,]1 [.]1 [A]2 [B]2 [C]2 [D]2 [E]6 [F]2 [H]1
[I]4 [L]1 [M]1 [N]2 [O]5 [R]1 [S]4 [T]6 [U]1 [Y]1
[A]1 [B]1 [E]2 [G]1 [L]2 [O]1 [P]1 [R]2 [V]1 [—]1

**WHEN CHOOSING THE
LESSER OF TWO EVILS,
REMEMBER IT'S STILL
AN EVIL. — MAX LERNER**
[']1 [,]1 [.]1 [A]1 [B]1 [C]1 [E]9 [F]1 [G]1 [H]3
[I]5 [L]5 [M]2 [N]3 [O]4 [R]3 [S]6 [T]4 [V]2 [W]2
[A]1 [E]2 [L]1 [M]1 [N]1 [R]2 [X]1 [—]1

**THE FEAR OF
THE LORD IS THE
BEGINNING OF WISDOM.
— PSALM 111:10**
[—]1 [.]1 [0]1 [1]4 [:]1 [A]2 [B]1 [D]2 [E]5 [F]3 [G]2
[H]3 [I]4 [L]2 [M]2 [N]3 [O]4 [P]1 [R]2 [S]3 [T]3 [W]1

Warm Welcomes
To Potential Parishioners

La casa de Dios es su casa

**VISIT OUR
SUPER SAVIOR CENTER.**
 [.]1 [A]1 [C]1 [E]3 [I]3 [N]1
 [O]2 [P]1 [R]4 [S]3 [T]2 [U]2 [V]2

**TURN RIGHT FOR
PUBLIC ACCESS TO
GOD'S KINGDOM.**
 [']1 [.]1 [A]1 [B]1 [C]3 [D]2 [E]1 [F]1 [G]3 [H]1
 [I]3 [K]1 [L]1 [M]1 [N]2 [O]4 [P]1 [R]3 [S]3 [T]3 [U]2

(or, depending on the sign's relation to the church entrance)

**TURN LEFT FOR
PUBLIC ACCESS TO
GOD'S KINGDOM.**
 [']1 [.]1 [A]1 [B]1 [C]3 [D]2 [E]2 [F]2 [G]2 [I]2
 [K]1 [L]2 [M]1 [N]2 [O]4 [P]1 [R]2 [S]3 [T]3 [U]2

**HOME TO SEVERAL REAL
SAINTS. CLASSES
OFFERED WEEKLY FOR
THE REST OF US.**
 [.]2 [A]4 [C]1 [D]1 [E]11 [F]4 [H]2 [I]1 [K]1 [L]4
 [M]1 [N]1 [O]5 [R]5 [S]8 [T]4 [U]1 [V]1 [W]1 [Y]1

195

FIND:GOD@TH;S/CHURCH.
    [.]1 [/]1 [:]1 [;]1 [@]1 [C]2 [D]2 [F]1
    [G]1 [H]3 [I]1 [N]1 [O]1 [R]1 [S]1 [T]1 [U]1

**WE'VE GOT A
PEW HERE WITH
YOUR NAME ON IT.**
    [']1 [.]1 [A]2 [E]6 [G]1 [H]2 [I]2 [M]1
    [N]2 [O]3 [P]1 [R]2 [T]3 [U]1 [V]1 [W]3 [Y]1

**SOFTLY AND TENDERLY
JESUS IS CALLING.**
    [.]1 [A]2 [C]1 [D]2 [E]3 [F]1 [G]1 [I]2
    [J]1 [L]4 [N]3 [O]1 [R]1 [S]4 [T]2 [U]1 [Y]2

**JOIN US FOR REAL
LIVE PREACHING
THIS SUNDAY.**
    [.]1 [A]3 [C]1 [D]1 [E]3 [F]1 [G]1 [H]2 [I]4 [J]1
    [L]2 [N]3 [O]2 [P]1 [R]3 [S]3 [T]1 [U]2 [V]1 [Y]1

COME AGAIN?
    [?]1 [A]2 [C]1 [E]1
    [G]1 [I]1 [M]1 [N]1 [O]1

**THIS IS A GREAT PLACE
FOR THOSE WHO WANT TO
BE ROOTED IN THE WORD,
NOT STUMPED BY IT.**
    [,]1 [.]1 [A]4 [B]2 [C]1 [D]3 [E]7 [F]1 [G]1 [H]4 [I]4
    [L]1 [M]1 [N]3 [O]8 [P]2 [R]4 [S]4 [T]10 [U]1 [W]3 [Y]1

COME JOIN OUR
LOST AND FOUND
COLLECTION.

[.]1 [A]1 [C]3 [D]2 [E]2 [F]1 [I]2 [J]1
[L]3 [M]1 [N]4 [O]7 [R]1 [S]1 [T]2 [U]2

COME IN FOR A
FREE MAKEOVER
THIS SUNDAY.

[.]1 [A]3 [C]1 [D]1 [E]5 [F]2 [H]1 [I]2 [K]1
[M]2 [N]2 [O]3 [R]3 [S]2 [T]1 [U]1 [V]1 [Y]1

MORE SONGS.
MORE WORSHIP.
MORE THAN JUST CHURCH.

[.]3 [A]1 [C]2 [E]3 [G]1 [H]4 [I]1 [J]1
[M]3 [N]2 [O]5 [P]1 [R]5 [S]4 [T]2 [U]2 [W]1

THIS IS THE
PERFECT PLACE FOR
IMPERFECT PEOPLE.

[.]1 [A]1 [C]3 [E]8 [F]3 [H]2 [I]3
[L]2 [M]1 [O]2 [P]5 [R]3 [S]2 [T]4

YOU DON'T HAVE TO
DRESS TO THE NINES
TO WORSHIP THE ONE.

[']1 [.]1 [A]1 [D]2 [E]6 [H]4 [I]2 [N]4
[O]7 [P]1 [R]2 [S]4 [T]6 [U]1 [V]1 [W]1 [Y]1

LONG TIME NO SEE?
[?]1 [E]3 [G]1 [I]1 [L]1
[M]1 [N]2 [O]2 [S]1 [T]1

LOST AND FOUND
FOR WOUNDED HEARTS.
[.]1 [A]2 [D]4 [E]2 [F]2 [H]1 [L]1
[N]3 [O]4 [R]2 [S]2 [T]2 [U]2 [W]1

FOR THOSE WHO'D NEVER
DARKEN A CHURCH
DOOR, WE'VE GOT SOME
NICE BIG WINDOWS.
[']2 [,]1 [.]1 [A]2 [B]1 [C]3 [D]4 [E]8 [F]1 [G]2 [H]4
[I]3 [K]1 [M]1 [N]4 [O]8 [R]5 [S]3 [T]2 [U]1 [V]2 [W]4

DON'T MAKE YOURSELF
A STRANGER.
[']1 [.]1 [A]3 [D]1 [E]3 [F]1 [G]1 [K]1
[L]1 [M]1 [N]2 [O]2 [R]3 [S]2 [T]2 [U]1 [Y]1

THERE'S ALWAYS ROOM
FOR ONE MORE
IN GOD'S HOUSE.
[']2 [.]1 [A]2 [D]1 [E]5 [F]1 [G]1 [H]2 [I]1
[L]1 [M]2 [N]2 [O]7 [R]4 [S]4 [T]1 [U]1 [W]1 [Y]1

HUNGRY FOR
SOMETHING SWEET?
TRY ONE OF OUR
SUNDAYS. — ANONYMOUS
[.]1 [?]1 [A]1 [D]1 [E]4 [F]2 [G]2 [H]2 [I]1
[M]1 [N]4 [O]5 [R]4 [S]4 [T]3 [U]3 [W]1 [Y]3
[A]1 [M]1 [N]2 [O]2 [S]1 [U]1 [Y]1 [—]1

OFFERING AN ICU
FOR SAINTS
AND SINNERS.
[.]1 [A]3 [C]1 [D]1 [E]2 [F]3 [G]1
[I]4 [N]6 [O]2 [R]3 [S]4 [T]1 [U]1

YOU'RE NOT TOO BAD
TO COME IN. YOU'RE
NOT TOO GOOD TO
STAY OUT. — ANONYMOUS
[']2 [.]2 [A]2 [B]1 [C]1 [D]2 [E]3 [G]1
[I]1 [M]1 [N]3 [O]14 [R]2 [S]1 [T]8 [U]3 [Y]3
[A]1 [M]1 [N]2 [O]2 [S]1 [U]1 [Y]1 [—]1

THIS SUNDAY,
GET THE LOWDOWN
ON A HIGHER CALLING.
[,]1 [.]1 [A]3 [C]1 [D]2 [E]3 [G]3 [H]4 [I]3
[L]3 [N]4 [O]3 [R]1 [S]2 [T]3 [U]1 [W]2 [Y]1

WE'VE AN EMPTY SPOT
JUST YOUR SIZE.
[']1 [.]1 [A]1 [E]4 [I]1 [J]1 [M]1 [N]1 [O]2
[P]2 [R]1 [S]3 [T]3 [U]2 [V]1 [W]1 [Y]2 [Z]1

199

(for churches w/ bilingual services)

SPANISH, ENGLISH,
& GOD'S WORD
SPOKEN HERE.
　　[&]1 [']1 [,]2 [.]1 [A]1 [D]2 [E]4 [G]2 [H]3
　　[I]2 [K]1 [L]1 [N]3 [O]3 [P]2 [R]2 [S]5 [W]1

(to announce pizza party)

PIZZA? PIZZA?
JESUS! JESUS!
　　[!]2 [?]2 [A]2 [E]2 [I]2
　　[J]2 [P]2 [S]4 [U]2 [Z]4

COME IN!
TAKE A LOAD
OF GUILT OFF!
　　[!]2 [A]3 [C]1 [D]1 [E]2 [F]3 [G]1
　　[I]2 [K]1 [L]2 [M]1 [N]1 [O]4 [T]2 [U]1

COME IN AND GET A
PEACE OF THE ROCK.
　　[.]1 [A]3 [C]3 [D]1 [E]5 [F]1 [G]1 [H]1
　　[I]1 [K]1 [M]1 [N]2 [O]3 [P]1 [R]1 [T]2

YOU'RE WELCOME.
　　[']1 [.]1 [C]1 [E]3 [L]1 [M]1
　　[O]2 [R]1 [U]1 [W]1 [Y]1

WE CHECK
OUR EGOS
AT THE DOOR.
[.]1 [A]1 [C]2 [D]1 [E]4 [G]1 [H]2
[K]1 [O]4 [R]2 [S]1 [T]2 [U]1 [W]1

When The Roll Is Called

*Admonitions on attendance to the
finding-it-hard-to-be faithful*

**LET US BREAK
THE BREAD OF
LIFE TOGETHER.**

[.]1 [A]2 [B]2 [D]1 [E]7 [F]2 [G]1 [H]2
[I]1 [K]1 [L]2 [O]2 [R]3 [S]1 [T]4 [U]1

**THERE'S MORE TO
CHURCH WHEN
YOU'RE HERE.**

[']2 [.]1 [C]2 [E]7 [H]5 [M]1 [N]1
[O]3 [R]5 [S]1 [T]2 [U]2 [W]1 [Y]1

**WE'VE GOT CHILDREN'S
CHURCH BECAUSE WE
REALLY KNOW HOW
TO KID AROUND.**

[']2 [.]1 [A]3 [B]1 [C]4 [D]3 [E]7 [G]1 [H]4 [I]2
[K]2 [L]3 [N]3 [O]5 [R]4 [S]2 [T]2 [U]3 [V]1 [W]4 [Y]1

**PASTOR'S GOT A
SERMON SIMMERING,
AND HE'S COOKING
FOR A CROWD.**

[']2 [,]1 [.]1 [A]4 [C]2 [D]2 [E]3 [F]1 [G]3 [H]1
[I]3 [K]1 [M]3 [N]4 [O]7 [P]1 [R]5 [S]5 [T]2 [W]1

FOR THE LOVE OF GOD,
COME TO CHURCH.
    [,]1 [.]1 [C]3 [D]1 [E]3 [F]2 [G]1
    [H]3 [L]1 [M]1 [O]6 [R]2 [T]2 [U]1 [V]1

IT'S NOT
JUST CHURCH.
IT'S FUN.
    [']2 [.]2 [C]2 [F]1 [H]2 [I]2
    [J]1 [N]2 [O]1 [R]1 [S]3 [T]4 [U]3

(to be used with a sign elevated at least ten feet)

MUST BE THIS
TALL TO MISS
SUNDAY SCHOOL.
    [.]1 [A]2 [B]1 [C]1 [D]1 [E]1 [H]2 [I]2
    [L]3 [M]2 [N]1 [O]3 [S]6 [T]4 [U]2 [Y]1

NOW OFFERING
AN EXTENDED
GRACE PERIOD.
    [.]1 [A]2 [C]1 [D]3 [E]6 [F]2 [G]2
    [I]2 [N]4 [O]3 [P]1 [R]3 [T]1 [W]1 [X]1

IF YOU CAN READ
THIS, YOU'RE CLOSE
ENOUGH TO COME IN.
    [']1 [,]1 [.]1 [A]2 [C]3 [D]1 [E]5 [F]1 [G]1 [H]2
    [I]3 [L]1 [M]1 [N]3 [O]6 [R]2 [S]2 [T]2 [U]3 [Y]2

EARLY TO BED,
EARLY TO RISE.
GO TO SUNDAY SCHOOL,
AND YOU'LL BE WISE.

[']1 [,]2 [.]2 [A]4 [B]2 [C]1 [D]3 [E]6 [G]1 [H]1
[I]2 [L]5 [N]2 [O]7 [R]3 [S]4 [T]3 [U]2 [W]1 [Y]4

THE BEST PART
OF WAKING UP
IS SUNDAY SCHOOL.

[.]1 [A]3 [B]1 [C]1 [D]1 [E]2 [F]1 [G]1 [H]2 [I]2
[K]1 [L]1 [N]2 [O]3 [P]2 [R]1 [S]4 [T]3 [U]2 [W]1 [Y]1

BREAD OF LIFE
MADE FRESH WEEKLY.

[.]1 [A]2 [B]1 [D]2 [E]6 [F]3 [H]1 [I]1
[K]1 [L]2 [M]1 [O]1 [R]2 [S]1 [W]1 [Y]1

YOUR P.I.T. STOP:
PRAISE
INSPIRATION
TEACHING

[.]3 [:]1 [A]3 [C]1 [E]2 [G]1 [H]1 [I]6
[N]3 [O]3 [P]4 [R]3 [S]3 [T]4 [U]1 [Y]1

(*Be sure to align the* P *in* PRAISE, *the* I *in* INSPIRATION, *and the* T *in* TEACHING.)

WHEREVER YOU GO,
THERE YOU ARE.
COME TO CHURCH!

[!]1 [,]1 [.]1 [A]1 [C]3 [E]7 [G]1 [H]4
[M]1 [O]5 [R]5 [T]2 [U]3 [V]1 [W]1 [Y]2

THERE'S A SWEET,
SWEET SPIRIT
IN THIS PLACE.

[']1 [,]1 [.]1 [A]2 [C]1 [E]7 [H]2
[I]4 [L]1 [N]1 [P]2 [R]2 [S]5 [T]5 [W]2

THE EARLY BIRD GETS
THE WORD. COME
TO SUNDAY SCHOOL.

[.]2 [A]2 [B]1 [C]2 [D]3 [E]5 [G]1 [H]3 [I]1
[L]2 [M]1 [N]1 [O]5 [R]3 [S]3 [T]4 [U]1 [W]1 [Y]2

RUN, DO NOT WALK,
TO YOUR NEAREST CHURCH.
THIS IS NOT A DRILL.

[,]2 [.]2 [A]3 [C]2 [D]2 [E]2 [H]3 [I]3 [K]1
[L]3 [N]4 [O]5 [R]5 [S]3 [T]5 [U]3 [W]1 [Y]1

OUR CHOIR
WILL STRIKE
A CHORD WITH YOU.

(*Note: Can substitute song service or musical*)
[.]1 [A]1 [C]2 [D]1 [E]1 [H]3 [I]4 [K]1
[L]2 [O]4 [R]4 [S]1 [T]2 [U]2 [W]2 [Y]1

HAVING A GOOD TIME.
WISH YOU WERE HERE.

[.]2 [A]2 [D]1 [E]5 [G]2 [H]3 [I]3 [M]1
[N]1 [O]3 [R]2 [S]1 [T]1 [U]1 [V]1 [W]2 [Y]1

FREE TRIP TO HEAVEN.
DETAILS INSIDE.
— ANONYMOUS

[.]2 [A]2 [D]2 [E]6 [F]1 [H]1 [I]4
[L]1 [N]2 [O]1 [P]1 [R]2 [S]2 [T]3 [V]1
[A]1 [M]1 [N]2 [O]2 [S]1 [U]1 [Y]1 [—]1

DON'T GO AWAY
EMPTY-HEARTED.

[']1 [-]1 [.]1 [A]3 [D]2 [E]3 [G]1 [H]1
[M]1 [N]1 [O]2 [P]1 [R]1 [T]3 [W]1 [Y]2

STAINS REMOVED.
MINDS CLEANED.
SPIRITS MENDED.
LIVES ALTERED.

[.]4 [A]3 [C]1 [D]6 [E]9 [I]5 [L]3
[M]3 [N]4 [O]1 [P]1 [R]3 [S]6 [T]3 [V]2

JUST PEW IT.

[.]1 [E]1 [I]1 [J]1
[P]1 [S]1 [T]2 [U]1 [W]1

C-H- -R-C-H
WE'RE MISSING U!

[!]1 [']1 [-]5 [C]2 [E]2 [G]1 [H]2
[I]2 [M]1 [N]1 [R]2 [S]2 [U]1 [W]1

**CHURCH MEMBERS ARE
LIKE CARS. THEY
USUALLY START MISSING
BEFORE THEY QUIT.**
[.]2 [A]4 [B]2 [C]3 [E]8 [F]1 [G]1 [H]4 [I]4 [K]1
[L]3 [M]3 [N]1 [O]1 [Q]1 [R]6 [S]6 [T]5 [U]4 [Y]3

**WHY WAIT 'TIL
THE ELEVENTH HOUR?
COME TO
SUNDAY SCHOOL, TOO.**
[']1 [,]1 [.]1 [?]1 [A]2 [C]2 [D]1 [E]5 [H]5 [I]2
[L]3 [M]1 [N]2 [O]7 [R]1 [S]2 [T]6 [U]2 [V]1 [W]2 [Y]2

Epilogue

Where do we go from here?

**WITH THE PROMISE
OF ETERNITY,
WHO NEEDS
HAPPY HOUR?**
[,]1 [?]1 [A]1 [D]1 [E]6 [F]1 [H]5 [I]3 [M]1
[N]2 [O]4 [P]3 [R]3 [S]2 [T]4 [U]1 [W]2 [Y]2

**NEVER REGRET GROWING
OLDER. IT'S A
PRIVILEGE DENIED TO
MANY. — ANONYMOUS**
[']1 [.]2 [A]2 [D]3 [E]9 [G]4 [I]5 [L]2 [M]1
[N]4 [O]3 [P]1 [R]6 [S]1 [T]3 [V]2 [W]1 [Y]1
[A]1 [M]1 [N]2 [O]2 [S]1 [U]1 [Y]1 [—]1

WHERE ARE YOU GOING?
[?]1 [A]1 [E]3 [G]2 [H]1 [I]1
[N]1 [O]2 [R]2 [U]1 [W]1 [Y]1

**EXERCISE YOUR FAITH
RATHER THAN GOING
FOR THE BURN.**
[.]1 [A]3 [B]1 [C]1 [E]5 [F]2 [G]2 [H]4
[I]3 [N]3 [O]3 [R]6 [S]1 [T]4 [U]2 [X]1 [Y]1

DON'T MISS HEAVEN
FOR ANYTHING
IN THIS WORLD.
[']1 [.]1 [A]2 [D]2 [E]2 [F]1 [G]1 [H]3 [I]4
[L]1 [M]1 [N]5 [O]3 [R]2 [S]3 [T]3 [V]1 [W]1 [Y]1

ON EARTH THERE IS NO
HEAVEN, BUT THERE
ARE PIECES OF IT.
— JULES RENARD
[,]1 [.]1 [A]3 [B]1 [C]1 [E]10 [F]1 [H]4
[I]3 [N]3 [O]3 [P]1 [R]4 [S]2 [T]5 [U]1 [V]1
[A]1 [D]1 [E]2 [J]1 [L]1 [N]1 [R]2 [S]1 [U]1 [—]1

WE RACE,
NOT AGAINST TIME,
BUT AGAINST
THE END OF IT.
[,]2 [.]1 [A]5 [B]1 [C]1 [D]1 [E]5 [F]1 [G]2
[H]1 [I]4 [M]1 [N]4 [O]2 [R]1 [S]2 [T]7 [U]1 [W]1

THE AFTERLIFE
HAS ITS
UPS AND DOWNS.
[.]1 [A]3 [D]2 [E]3 [F]2 [H]2 [I]2 [L]1
[N]2 [O]1 [P]1 [R]1 [S]4 [T]3 [U]1 [W]1

GOING UP?
[?]1 [G]2 [I]1
[N]1 [O]1 [P]1 [U]1

TO GET TO HEAVEN,
TURN RIGHT AND
KEEP STRAIGHT.
— ANONYMOUS
[,]1 [.]1 [A]3 [D]1 [E]5 [G]3 [H]3 [I]2
[K]1 [N]3 [O]2 [P]1 [R]3 [S]1 [T]7 [U]1 [V]1
[A]1 [M]1 [N]2 [O]2 [S]1 [U]1 [Y]1 [—]1

IN THE END, IT'S
A JUDGMENT CALL.
[']1 [,]1 [.]1 [A]2 [C]1 [D]2 [E]3 [G]1
[H]1 [I]2 [J]1 [L]2 [M]1 [N]3 [S]1 [T]3 [U]1

SIN AND BEAR IT.
[.]1 [A]2 [B]1 [D]1 [E]1
[I]2 [N]2 [R]1 [S]1 [T]1

THE FAST LANE COULD
BE A HIGHWAY TO HELL.
[.]1 [A]4 [B]1 [C]1 [D]1 [E]4 [F]1 [G]1 [H]4
[I]1 [L]4 [N]1 [O]2 [S]1 [T]3 [U]1 [W]1 [Y]1

FOR NOW, WE'RE CAUGHT
BETWEEN THE THIRD ROCK
AND A HEAVENLY PLACE.
[']1 [,]1 [.]1 [A]5 [B]1 [C]3 [D]2 [E]9 [F]1 [G]1 [H]4
[I]1 [K]1 [L]2 [N]4 [O]3 [P]1 [R]4 [T]4 [U]1 [V]1 [W]3 [Y]1

EVEN IF HEAVEN BOGGLES
THE MIND, MOST HEARTS
DON'T HAVE
A PROBLEM WITH IT.
[']1 [,]1 [.]1 [A]4 [B]2 [D]2 [E]9 [F]1 [G]2 [H]5
[I]4 [L]2 [M]3 [N]4 [O]4 [P]1 [R]2 [S]3 [T]6 [V]3 [W]1

HEAVEN OR BUST.
[.]1 [A]1 [B]1 [E]2 [H]1 [N]1
[O]1 [R]1 [S]1 [T]1 [U]1 [V]1

SIN CAN THRILL
YOU TO DEATH.
[.]1 [A]2 [C]1 [D]1 [E]1 [H]2 [I]2
[L]2 [N]2 [O]2 [R]1 [S]1 [T]3 [U]1 [Y]1

HEAVEN WILL BE PERFECT
— NO MONDAYS.
[—]1 [.]1 [A]2 [B]1 [C]1 [D]1 [E]5 [F]1 [H]1 [I]1
[L]2 [M]1 [N]3 [O]2 [P]1 [R]1 [S]1 [T]1 [V]1 [W]1 [Y]1

HELL'S THE PITS.
[']1 [.]1 [E]2 [H]2 [I]1
[L]2 [P]1 [S]2 [T]2

IF IT'S
THE RAPTURE,
WE'RE OUTTA HERE.
[']2 [,]1 [.]1 [A]2 [E]6 [F]1 [H]2
[I]2 [O]1 [P]1 [R]4 [S]1 [T]5 [U]2 [W]1

**LIFE ON EARTH IS
NO BED OF ROSES,
BUT YOU CAN SLEEP
IT OFF IN HEAVEN.**

[,]1 [.]1 [A]3 [B]2 [C]1 [D]1 [E]8 [F]4 [H]2 [I]4
[L]2 [N]5 [O]6 [P]1 [R]2 [S]4 [T]3 [U]2 [V]1 [Y]1

**HEAVEN'S
A BLESSING
IN DA SKIES.**

[']1 [.]1 [A]3 [B]1 [D]1 [E]4 [G]1
[H]1 [I]3 [K]1 [L]1 [N]3 [S]5 [V]1

**TWO-WAY ROAD AHEAD.
CHOOSE WISELY.**

[-]1 [.]2 [A]4 [C]1 [D]2 [E]3 [H]2
[I]1 [L]1 [O]4 [R]1 [S]2 [T]1 [W]3 [Y]2